Teacher's Manual

JUMP Math
Confidence Building Units

MW01536623

Fractions Challenge — Level C, D

Contents

This manual accompanies the
Fractions Challenge (Level C) and the
Fractions Challenge (Level D).

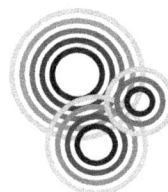

jump math
MULTIPLYING POTENTIAL.

JUMP Math
One Yonge Street, Suite 1014
Toronto, Ontario M5E 1E5
Canada
www.jumpmath.org

Writer: John Mighton
Layout: Linh Lam, Gabriella Kerr

ISBN: 978-1-927457-26-9

Printed and bound in Canada

THE PURPOSE OF THE CONFIDENCE BUILDING UNIT: Introduction by John Mighton

In the twenty-five years I have spent teaching mathematics to children, I have never met an educator who would say that students who lack confidence in their intellectual or academic abilities are likely to do well in school. Unfortunately, programs of mathematics used in our public schools rarely take proper account of the role of confidence in learning. If students are more apt to do well in a subject when they believe they are capable of doing well, it seems clear that any math program that aims to harness the potential of every student should start with an exercise that will build the confidence of every student.

The *Fractions Challenge* Confidence Building Unit was designed for exactly this purpose: it has proven to be an extremely effective tool for convincing even the most challenged student that they can do well in mathematics. (For detailed research on this unit, see the "JUMP for Joy!" report on our website.)

While many teachers and JUMP volunteers have had considerable success using the *Fractions Challenge* Confidence Building Unit in one-on-one tutorials, the unit has often had its greatest effect in the classroom. When weaker students are allowed to succeed in front of their peers, when they can raise their hands confidently in class, knowing that they are capable of answering the same questions as the faster students, when they can work independently without fear of failure, and can experience the thrill of completing work that is considered beyond their grade level (without constantly asking their teacher for help or copying from their peers), they are often transformed by the experience (and often cease to be weaker students).

This unit does not teach fractions in depth. To teach fractions in depth, you can use the lesson plans in the regular JUMP *Teacher Resources*. The purpose of this unit is solely to convince your weaker students that they can meet difficult-looking challenges (so they will focus more and persevere in their work) and to allow all students to benefit from the excitement that can sweep through a class when all students feel they are capable of learning math.

The individual steps you will follow in teaching the material in this unit are extremely small, so that even the weakest students needn't be left behind; but the method of instruction is not rote. Throughout the unit, students are expected to:
- ✓ discover or extend patterns or rules on their own,
- ✓ see what changes and what stays the same in sequences of mathematical expressions, and
- ✓ apply chains of inference or computation in new situations.

Students become very excited at making these discoveries and meeting these challenges as they learn the material. For many students, it is the first time they have ever been motivated to pay attention to mathematical rules and patterns or to try to extend their knowledge to new cases.

The various steps you will follow in teaching the material in this unit are outlined in great detail below, and also on the worksheets themselves. The individual steps are never more difficult than "count on your fingers" or "copy this symbol from here to here," so the steps themselves will never be a barrier to weaker students. If you follow the instructions in this manual very closely, even your weakest students should achieve a mark of 80% or higher on the final diagnostic test.

If you do not believe that all of your students can do well on the final test, then you should reconsider your decision to use the *Fractions Challenge* Confidence Building Unit: the performance of your weaker students will almost certainly match your expectations. It is certainly possible that you

have a student in your class who simply cannot learn the material in the *Fractions Challenge* Confidence Building Unit, but the odds of this are extremely low. I have taught the unit to hundreds of students, even in very low remedial classes, and have yet to meet a child in the regular school system in Grades 3 to 6 who couldn't learn the material in this unit. As well, dozens of independent implementations of this unit have shown that, with very few exceptions, even the most challenged students can score over 80% on their first try at the unit test. As the point of this unit is primarily to inspire confidence in your weakest students, there is little point in teaching the unit if you are not willing to try to teach to this goal. If you find you are leaving students behind in the unit, you may be making one of the mistakes listed in the section "Common Errors Made in Teaching the Confidence Building Unit" on page 9.

We recommend that you teach the material in this unit for two weeks at most. If you don't finish the unit, modify the final test so that it only contains material that you covered.

Why Start with Fractions Rather than a Different Topic in Mathematics?

Even if you agree that it is important to start your math program with an exercise that will build the confidence of your weaker students, you may wonder why you should teach those students material on fractions that is beyond the current expectations for the elementary curriculum. Although JUMP staff and participating teachers have used the *Fractions Challenge* Confidence Building Unit with great success for over five years now, I have only recently begun to fully understand why the unit has such a significant impact on students. To be effective, any unit that aims to increase the confidence of students must, in my opinion, meet certain criteria. To help you teach the *Fractions Challenge* Confidence Building Unit with understanding and conviction, I have provided a list of these criteria below and I have indicated how I think the unit meets them:

Criteria #1
Any exercise that aims to build the confidence of weaker students must only require that students possess a very small set of skills to complete their work successfully. It must be possible to teach these skills even to the most challenged students in a short time. And a teacher must be able to verify easily that every student in their class has acquired the necessary skills before they start the exercise.

In a typical public school, even in Grade 3, an enormous gap in knowledge, ability and motivation exists between the weakest and strongest students. Any exercise that aims to build the confidence of weaker students must take account of this gap. The exercise should not demand too much of weaker students, or the purpose of the exercise will be defeated right from the start.

To achieve a perfect score on the final Unit test, your students need only possess three skills: they must be able to skip count on their fingers (by 2's, 3's and 5's on one hand only) and they must be able to add and subtract one-digit numbers (on their fingers if necessary). A method of teaching these three skills, which has been proven to work extremely well even with remedial students, is outlined in Section F-1 and in the Appendix. **Before you start the Confidence Building Unit, you should take the time to verify that all of your students have the skills they need to do well in the unit.**

Criteria #2
In classrooms where mathematics has been taught in a traditional way, students usually work at very different speeds. To keep students who are initially faster from getting bored, an exercise that seeks to build the confidence of weaker students must provide (or show teachers how to design) extra work for students who finish early.

If a student can add and subtract one-digit numbers and multiply by 2's, 3's, and 5's on one hand, then they should be able to complete any of the *Fractions Challenge* Confidence Building Unit worksheets that are marked with an *A* in the upper right-hand corner of the page. When every student in your class has finished the *A* worksheet for a particular section, you should move on to the next section. You should not expect all of your students to finish the *B* or *C* pages for a given section: these pages contain extra work that can be assigned to faster students to allow you time to verify that every one of your students have answered the questions on the *A* page correctly.

The questions on the *B* and *C* pages are always on exactly the same topic as the questions on the preceding *A* page, but usually require that students multiply and divide by numbers greater than 2, 3 or 5. Do not allow a student to work on a *B* or *C* page unless you are sure they know the times tables required for that page (or unless you have written the tables up on the board).

If you create bonus questions of your own for faster students, your goal should be to gain time to work with students who need extra help. If the bonus questions you create introduce a new topic or are too difficult, you may end up having to help students who could otherwise be working independently while you pay attention to more needy students. (That is why the bonus questions on the *B* and *C* pages are always on the same topic as those on the *A* pages.) As you become more experienced at creating bonus questions, you will see that for any topic in mathematics it is very easy to create questions that are only incrementally harder than the regular work, but that look a great deal harder. For instance, if a child can add $\frac{1}{2} + \frac{1}{3} + \frac{1}{6}$, ask them to add $\frac{1}{2} + \frac{1}{3} + \frac{1}{6} + \frac{1}{12}$ or $\frac{1}{2} + \frac{1}{3} + \frac{1}{6} + \frac{1}{12} + \frac{1}{60}$.

(Of course there will be times in your math program when you may want your faster students to explore more challenging topics on their own. But bear in mind that the goal of the *Fractions Challenge* Confidence Building Unit is to build the confidence of weaker students: for this purpose you should find that the bonus questions provided are sufficient to keep faster students busy.)

You should not underestimate how excited your faster students will become at answering bonus questions, even when those questions are only incrementally harder than the regular work. Children love showing off to a caring adult: if you become excited when you assign the bonus questions then your faster students will become excited about solving them. And this excitement will spill over to the slower students as well. In every class where I have taught the *Fractions Challenge* Confidence Building Unit, the slower students have always started racing through their worksheets so that they could be assigned bonus questions too. (And often kids who were initially slower started out-pacing kids who were initially faster.)

I always make up special bonus questions for the most challenged students too, so they can feel that they are doing harder work as well. For instance, when a weaker student can add the triple fractions with the same denominator on worksheet F-4 A, I will say "Do you think you can handle four fractions?" and write $\frac{1}{17} + \frac{1}{17} + \frac{1}{17} + \frac{1}{17}$ across the bottom of their page. I have yet to encounter a student who didn't respond enthusiastically to this kind of challenge.

All of the teachers who took part in a JUMP pilot last year affirmed on surveys that their stronger students were not bored during the *Fractions Challenge* Confidence Building Unit. Those teachers also acknowledged that they had underestimated (and in many cases greatly underestimated) the ability of their weaker students to keep up with the stronger students! (For details, see the "JUMP for Joy!" report available online.)

Criteria #3

An exercise that seeks to build the confidence of weaker students must recognize that for many children (especially in inner-city schools) language can be a barrier to mathematics.

As a mathematician, I believe that students should be taught to explain and discuss mathematical ideas. But based on my experience teaching hundreds of children, I also believe that exercises that demand a substantial amount of reading and writing should be introduced into the elementary mathematical curriculum very carefully and incrementally. Before children can read and write fluently, they must acquire an enormous number of visual, motor, auditory and cognitive skills. In mathematics, on the other hand, even concepts used by working mathematicians can be reduced to one of two extremely basic operations, namely the operation of counting or the operation of grouping objects into sets. (Logicians proved this over a hundred years ago.) As the vast majority of children are able to perform these operations long before they become expert readers, mathematics is the one subject in which the majority of kids are naturally equipped to excel at an early age. If we were to allow all kids to achieve their full potential in mathematics (by removing language as a barrier to learning the subject), I am certain that the sense of confidence and focus, as well as the conceptual abilities children would develop in that subject, would have an effect in other subjects.

To elaborate, this is not to say that children should not be taught to explain their work or communicate about mathematical ideas: in the grade-specific JUMP workbooks, these skills are taught incrementally in a very rigorous and effective way.

Many teachers who have used the *Fractions Challenge* Confidence Building Unit have reported significant improvements in their students' ability to concentrate and to focus on printed materials, as well as in their ability to see patterns, to perceive what changes and what stays the same in a sequence of symbols, to follow chains of inference, and to generalize and extend rules to new cases. These are exactly the skills that a child must possess in order to become a fluent reader.

In our public education system, we now try to teach reading and literacy at the expense of mathematics by loading too much language into our elementary textbooks. By neglecting to ever teach elementary students math in a purer form, as a symbolic language in its own right, we neglect a tool that could help students become more literate. If we were to use less language in the early part of our math programs (and introduce it more carefully in the later part) and if we were to allow students to sometimes play math more as a game of manipulating symbols, generalizing rules and seeing patterns, I would predict that we could accelerate students' development as readers. (And we would undoubtedly allow children in inner-city schools to be far more successful at school: students who have English as a second language, or who are delayed in their reading, often fall behind in mathematics unnecessarily because of the language in the textbooks.)

To teach the *Fractions Challenge* Confidence Building Unit effectively, you should think of the unit – in part – as an exercise in reading (or a preparation for reading) for your weaker students. Rather than having to grapple with the 26 letters of the alphabet and a vast number of ill-defined rules for combining those letters, your students can experience mastery in a more simple symbolic universe that contains only a handful of symbols (i.e. the numerals from zero to nine as well as a few operation signs) and a handful of rules for combining those symbols. You should not underestimate the degree to which manipulating these mathematical symbols mentally, and copying and lining the symbols up properly on the page, will affect your weaker students as readers and as writers.

I was invited to speak at the Hospital for Sick Children in Toronto in 2004, after teaching the *Fractions Challenge* Confidence Building Unit to a very challenged nine-year-old boy: his doctor invited me to talk to a group of specialists on childhood development because he had noticed remarkable changes in the boy, not only in ability and attitude, but also in handwriting skills. According to the boy's doctor and mother, the boy could learn cursive letters much more quickly after completing the unit. I have noticed similar changes in handwriting and motor skills in other students who have completed the unit. In the *Fractions Challenge* Confidence Building Unit, students are required to constantly organize sequences of symbols on the page, while having to look for patterns and to remember and generalize rules. At the same time, they are in a state of extreme excitement at being able to do advanced work and at being offered the opportunity to show off to a caring adult. I believe that the combination of these factors is what causes so many changes in weaker students: each factor on its own would not have the same effect.

Criteria #4
Whenever new concepts or new rules or operations are introduced, the teacher must be able to quickly verify that every student has understood the new material. And the teacher must find it easy to provide remediation quickly and efficiently for students who need extra help.

Textbooks and programs of mathematics are rarely designed to take account of the difficulties teachers face in large classrooms. Current philosophies of education advocate that children be encouraged to explore and discover mathematical ideas in somewhat open-ended problem solving lessons. While I agree with this approach as one of the goals in math education, I also believe that it is a mistake to start a math program with too many lessons of this kind. Children who struggle with math, or who have trouble focusing, are usually left behind by this kind of teaching.

Problem-solving lessons, particularly those involving manipulatives, must be very carefully designed to ensure that every student is engaged and none are left behind. In some of the inner-city classes I have observed, I have seen children spend more time arguing over who had what colour of block or who had more blocks than they spent concentrating on the lesson. Students need to be confident, focused and motivated to do productive work with manipulatives. In JUMP we begin with the *Fractions Challenge* Confidence Building Unit (in which students are expected to work independently with pencil and paper) to allow students to develop the confidence and focus required for work with manipulatives. (The JUMP Teacher's Manuals for the grade-specific workbooks contain a number of effective problem-solving lessons with manipulatives that are introduced after the *Fractions Challenge* Confidence Building Unit.)

If teachers aim to engage all of their students (not just the ones who are more advanced than their peers), and if children must be confident and attentive to learn, then it seems obvious that the teacher must start their math program by assigning work that every student can complete without the help of their peers. When students work in groups with manipulatives, it is often hard to verify that every student has understood the lesson. The *Fractions Challenge* Confidence Building Unit is designed to allow teachers to identify and help students who need remediation immediately, so that every student gains the confidence they need to do more independent work. (Of course it's possible that a good teacher might design a unit with manipulatives that has the same effect with extremely challenged students as this unit.)

The various steps for teaching the operations in this unit are laid out in great detail in the manual and on the worksheets. As well, the manual contains a number of hints on how to help students who

struggle with a step. If you follow these guidelines carefully in teaching the unit, you should always be able to see where a student is struggling and provide the appropriate help.

NOTE: After looking at the *Fractions Challenge* Confidence Building Unit, some educators have suggested that JUMP does not advocate using concrete models to teach fractions: this misunderstanding of JUMP is based on an incomplete knowledge of our materials. The grade-specific JUMP workbooks are full of exercises with concrete materials and pictures that teach the connection between the abstract notation for quantities and operations involving fractions and the various concrete models for fractions. (In fact, I believe that the workbooks do a more complete job of teaching the connection between concrete and abstract representations of fractions than any elementary textbooks I have seen.) In teaching the *Fractions Challenge* Confidence Building Unit you should remember that its goal is not to teach students to fully understand the connection between the symbolic operations with fractions and the concrete models that underlie those operations (although some students do come out of the unit understanding the connection: we recommend that you always explain briefly, with a picture, as outlined in the manual, why the operations work). This unit is intended as a brief excursion into the symbolic world of mathematics: its point is not to explain fractions fully but to allow children to experience complete mastery in a rich and interesting abstract game. (You can teach students to understand fractions fully using our workbooks.)

We underestimate children by assuming that they will only enjoy learning concepts that have obvious physical models or applications. While I would encourage a teacher to serve pieces of pie or pizza to their class to illustrate a point about fractions, this is not the only way to get kids interested in math. Children will happily play a game with numbers or mathematical symbols, even if it has no obvious connection to the everyday world, as long as the game presents a series of interesting challenges, has clear rules and outcomes, and if the person playing the game has a good chance of winning. Children are born to solve puzzles: in my experience, they are completely happy at school if they are allowed to exercise their minds and to show off to a caring adult. What children hate most is failure. They generally find mathematical rules and operations boring only because those things are often poorly taught, without passion, in a manner that produces very few winners.

Some math educators, who may not understand the extent to which mathematics is a game of inventing and manipulating symbols, have assumed that children cannot possibly learn anything from the *Fractions Challenge* Confidence Building Unit because the unit does not emphasize concrete models. I will give one example to show how inaccurate this view is:

I recently came across the following question on a Grade 7 entrance exam for a school for gifted children:

If $a \lozenge b = a \times b + 3$, what does $4 \lozenge 5$ equal?

Most educators would probably say that this is a very good "conceptual" question for Grade 7 students. To solve the problem, a student must see which symbols change and which ones remain the same on either side of the equal sign in the equation. The letters a and b appear on both sides of the equal sign but, on the left-hand side, they are multiplied (then added to the number 3): once a student notices this, they can see that the solution to the problem is $4 \times 5 + 3 = 23$. The ability to see patterns of this sort in an equation and to see what changes – and what stays the same on either side of an equal sign – are essential skills in algebra.

When I teach the *Fractions Challenge* Confidence Building Unit, I start by showing students how to add a pairs of fractions with the same denominators: you add the numerators of the fractions while keeping the denominator the same. But then, without further explanation, I ask students how they would add three fractions with the same denominator. In other words, I ask:

If $\frac{1}{4} + \frac{1}{4} = \frac{2}{4}$, what does $\frac{1}{4} + \frac{1}{4} + \frac{1}{4}$ equal?

The logical structure of this question is very similar to the question from the enriched entrance exam: to find the answer, students have to notice that the number 4 remains unchanged in the denominators of the fractions and the numbers in the numerators are combined by addition. In my opinion, the question is "conceptual" in much the same way that the question on the entrance exam is conceptual.

The exercises in the *Fractions Challenge* Confidence Building Unit contain a good deal of subtle conceptual work of the sort found in the example above: in virtually every question, students are required to see what changes and what stays the same in an equation, to recognize and generalize patterns, to follow chains of inference and to extend rules to new cases (for many students, it is the first time they have ever been motivated to direct their attention to these sorts of things at school). But because the questions in the *Fractions Challenge* Confidence Building Unit are not generally formulated in terms of pie diagrams and fraction strips, many educators have had trouble seeing any value in this unit. (And no matter how often I point out that the regular JUMP worksheets contain lots of exercises with pattern blocks, pie diagrams and fraction strips, educators who believe that younger students shouldn't be taught any operations with fractions never seem to hear me.)

Criteria #5
An exercise that aims to build the confidence of weaker students must allow the teacher to raise the bar incrementally so students can experience the thrill of meeting a series of graduated mathematical challenges.

In my experience, difficult children respond much more quickly to praise and success than to criticism and threats. Of course, a teacher must be firm with students and must establish clear rules and boundaries, but I've found it's generally easier to get kids to adhere to rules and to respect others if they feel admired and successful.

I have worked with hundreds of children with attention deficits and behavioural problems over the past 15 years (even in the correctional system) and I have had a great deal of success changing behaviour using a simple technique: if I encounter a student who I think might cause problems in a class, I'll say: "You're very smart. I'd better give you something more challenging." Then I give the student a question that is only incrementally harder – or that only looks harder – than the one they are working on. For instance, if a student can add three fractions with the same denominator, I give them a question with four fractions. (I never give a challenge to a difficult student unless I'm certain they can do the question.) I always make sure, when the student succeeds in meeting my challenge, that they know I am impressed. Sometimes I even pretend to faint (students always laugh at this) or I will say: "You got that question but you'll never get the next one." Students become very excited when they succeed in meeting a series of graduated challenges. And their excitement allows them to focus their attention and make the leaps I have described in *The Myth of Ability*. (Of course you don't have to use my exact methods: teachers find different ways to praise their students, but I think passion is essential.)

The technique of raising the bar is very simple but it seems to work universally: I have used it in inner-city schools, in behavioural classes and even in the detention system, and I have yet to meet a student who didn't respond to it. Children universally enjoy exercising their minds and showing off to a caring adult.

Although JUMP covers the traditional curriculum, the program demands a radical change in the way teachers deliver the curriculum: JUMP is based on the idea that success is not a by-product of learning – it is the *very foundation* of learning. If you aren't willing to give difficult students graduated challenges that they can succeed at, and if you aren't willing to be excited at their successes, then we would implore you not to use JUMP.

In mathematics, it is extremely easy to raise the bar incrementally: I don't know of any other subject in which a teacher can break skills into such minute steps, and can gauge so precisely the size of the step and a student's readiness to attempt a new step. I believe there is no other subject in which it is easier to harness the attention and enthusiasm of difficult students.

I know that in a big class it's extremely hard to give attention to difficult students, but sometimes a few five-minute sessions spent giving a student a series of graduated challenges (that you know they can succeed at) can make all the difference to the student (and to your stress levels!).

NOTE: Once students develop a sense of confidence in math and know how to work independently, you can sometimes allow them to struggle more with challenges: students need to eventually learn that it's natural to fail on occasion and that solving problems sometimes takes a great deal of trial and error.

Criteria #6
An exercise that aims to build the confidence of weaker students should expose them to a body of knowledge that has a degree of unity (so students can see how skills and concepts they learned for one topic apply to another) and that is rich enough to allow students the experience of ascending through the levels of a rather substantial structure (like climbing a mountain and looking back at the series of cliffs you've scaled). It also helps if the material in the exercise is perceived by students to be difficult and advanced.

Fractions underlie all of mathematics and are generally thought to be impossible for some students to master. Many students first start to struggle in math when they are introduced to fractions. When elementary students see that they can do the work that older kids often struggle with, they become convinced that they are good at math.

In the *Fractions Challenge* Confidence Building Unit, one skill builds on another, so that students always have to think carefully about which method they should use for answering a question. For instance, after learning to add fractions by changing both denominators, students are taught to check if one denominator divides into the other in case they can add the fractions more efficiently. They then learn to extend this skill to add mixed and triple fractions.

Many math programs for weaker students consist of endless drills in basic skills. Because children who struggle in math are generally assumed to be incapable of doing more advanced work, they gradually lose all confidence and motivation so that, even after several years of extra help in math, they can scarcely remember the simplest facts. Many of the children who enter the JUMP program have not, after five or six years of regular school, managed to learn even the three times table. Based

on my observations of hundreds of students, I have come to believe that the best way to motivate children who have fallen behind is to skip them ahead – to convince them that they are capable of doing work beyond their grade level. The remarkable progress weaker students have made using the *Fractions Challenge* Confidence Building Unit shows the enormous role a student's perception plays in learning. Clearly, students learn more quickly if they feel they are doing advanced work and succeeding.

I first started teaching fractions to remedial students because I thought that it might motivate them to learn their times tables. A fact learned while practicing challenging mathematics is more readily recalled than one learned by rote drill: when students constantly have to multiply and divide in the course of adding and reducing fractions, they become extremely motivated to learn their times tables. Often students who were not previously inspired to do extra work will ask to learn higher times tables so they can work on the *B* and *C* sheets. (By the time your students are halfway through the unit you should show them how to count and multiply by 4's on one hand.)

Because the *Fractions Challenge* Confidence Building Unit contains material that is considered beyond the level of elementary students, it has proven to be an extremely effective tool for helping teachers discover a potential in their students that they might not otherwise have seen. In a recent pilot, all of the teachers who used this unit acknowledged that they had underestimated (or in many cases greatly underestimated) their weaker students in over ten categories, including enthusiasm, concentration, ability to remember number facts, willingness to ask for harder work, and ability to keep up with faster students. The teachers also acknowledged that the gains their students had made in mathematics spilled over into other subjects.

Common Errors Made in Teaching the Confidence Building Unit

- *Don't assume that a student who forgets material easily will never learn the material.*
  Even mathematicians constantly forget new material, including material they once understood completely. (I have forgotten things I discovered myself!) Children, like mathematicians, need a good deal of practice and frequent review in order to remember new material. (Also remember that the more excited you are at a student's progress and the more you use bonus questions to capture a student's attention, the more likely they will be to remember the things you teach them.)

  Whenever I have taught JUMP in a classroom for an extended time, I have found that I generally needed to set aside five minutes every few days to give extra review and preparation to the lowest four or five students in the class. (I usually teach these students in a small group while the other students are working on other activities.) Surprisingly, this is all it takes for the majority of students to keep up (of course, in extreme cases, it may not be enough).

  I know, given current class sizes and the amount of paperwork teachers are burdened with, that it's very hard for teachers to find extra time to devote to weaker students but, if you can find the time, you will see that it makes an enormous difference to these students and to the class in general. (By investing a little extra time in your weaker students, you may end up saving time as you won't have to deal so much with the extreme split in abilities that is common in most classes, or with the disruptive behaviour that students who have fallen behind often engage in.)

- *Do not introduce extraneous materials into the unit.*
  Bear in mind that students do not have to understand fractions completely in order to do well on the final test: they must simply master the skills taught in the unit. (Some educators think it's harmful to

teach children things they will only understand incompletely. While I agree with this principle in general, there are sometimes benefits to teaching children things they will only partially understand.)

REMEMBER: Fraction concepts are taught very thoroughly (with a variety of concrete materials and activities) in our grade-specific workbooks. The *Fractions Challenge* Confidence Building Unit is designed more to build confidence, harness attention and motivate children to learn their number facts than to teach fractions completely.

- *Emphasize the positive.*
  If a child gets three out of four questions wrong, I will mark the question that is correct first and praise them for getting the correct answer. Then I will say, "I think you didn't understand something with these other questions" or "You may have been going too fast," and then I will point out their mistake – or ask them to find it themselves! I've found that if I start by mentioning the mistakes, a weaker student will sometimes simply give up or stop listening. If a student is upset by their mistakes, I will sometimes make up a bonus question (that I know they can do) to show them they are capable of doing harder work. (I also tell students that even though I am a mathematician I often make mistakes. And I often start a lesson by telling students that if they don't understand something it is my fault for not explaining it well enough, so they shouldn't feel embarrassed at asking me to explain something again.)

- *Never allow students to work ahead of the section you are teaching.*
  If some students finish all of the bonus questions on the *B* and *C* sheets for a particular section before everyone else has finished the *A* page, make up extra bonus questions, encourage students to make up bonus questions for others or allow students to do independent work in another subject (for instance, silent reading.) If you allow some students to work ahead of the others in the worksheets, you will never be able to build the momentum and excitement that comes when an entire class experiences success together.

If you find you are leaving students behind you should ask:
- ✓ Can all of my students multiply without hesitation by 2's, 3's and 5's (as taught in Section F-1 of the unit)?
- ✓ Can all of my students add and subtract one-digit numbers (as taught in the Appendix to the Teacher's Manual for the *Fractions Challenge* Confidence Building Unit)?
- ✓ Am I being careful to isolate the most basic steps in the operations?
- ✓ Am I teaching one step at a time and allowing enough repetition?
- ✓ Am I following the hints given in the unit for teaching weaker students?
- ✓ Am I expecting my students to learn or remember things that aren't relevant to the steps I'm trying to teach?
- ✓ Am I building momentum in my lessons by allowing all of my students to succeed?
- ✓ Am I giving sufficient encouragement?
- ✓ Am I spending extra time with my weaker students and giving them extra practice?
- ✓ Am I excited about my students' progress?
- ✓ Do I believe that all of my students can learn mathematics?

You should allow your students to write a practice test before they write the final test or, alternatively, you should re-test students who don't score 80% or higher on their first test (after reviewing the material they struggled with).

The Role of Tutors

When you teach the *Fractions Challenge* Confidence Building Unit, it helps to have an assistant in the classroom for two or three lessons a week. With the help of an assistant, you can run a very dynamic lesson: after you teach a step at the blackboard, you and your assistant can circulate around the class writing words of encouragement on the students' workbooks (kids love phrases like "Great," "Wow" or "Excellent") and correcting students' mistakes. I've found it's fairly easy to get around the class and pay attention to each student if I have one assistant in a class of twenty-five kids. Kids love the instant feedback they get when there are enough people in the room to give them each a little extra attention.

A number of schools that have implemented JUMP independently have found various and innovative ways of providing teachers with tutorial assistance several times a week during the *Fractions Challenge* Confidence Building Unit:

✓ Some schools have used education assistants, Methods and Resource teachers, or interns from a local teacher's college as tutors.

✓ Some schools have used parents and local volunteers (a single volunteer can visit three or four classrooms in a morning, so it doesn't take many volunteers to run a JUMP program.)

✓ Some schools have integrated a special ed-class with a regular class and used one of the two teachers as a tutor.

✓ Some schools have used older students as tutors. (I think this is a particularly viable model. Many schools now have reading buddies and math buddies would ultimately be even more efficient than reading buddies, as a math buddy could help more than one child: in a JUMP-style lesson, a single math buddy – or several math buddies – could help an entire class.)

✓ Some teachers have even used peer tutors from their own class to help with marking. (If you use this kind of model, I would recommend that you occasionally give separate coaching to weaker students before a lesson so they can be tutors for the day.)

Although I haven't taught the *Fractions Challenge* Confidence Building Unit entirely without assistance, I believe it could be done. (I have taught many individual lessons without tutors.) To teach the unit without tutors, I would occasionally give five- or ten-minute coaching session to weaker students in small groups before more difficult lessons (so I could be sure those students could work independently during the lesson). And I would probably use peer tutors sometimes to generate excitement in the lesson. It is certainly easier, however, to teach the unit with the help of tutors. Many schools have shown that providing some tutorial support for teachers is well within a school's resources (particularly for the first few months of school, until weaker students start to catch up).

Note to One-on-One Tutors

If you are using the *Fractions Challenge* Confidence Building Unit once a week as part of an in-school or after school one-on-one program, I would recommend that you not spend more than 8 to 10 lessons on this unit (you can shorten the unit test to match what you have covered). It is important that you allow enough time in the year to teach from the grade-specific workbooks.

THE CONFIDENCE BUILDING UNIT

Section F-1: Counting

First check if your student can count on one hand by twos, threes and fives. If they can't, you will have to teach them. A simple way to do this is to draw a hand like this:

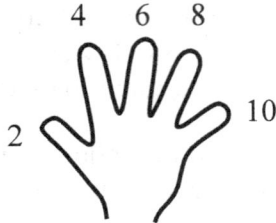

Have your student practise for a minute or two with the diagram, then without. When your student can count by twos, threes and fives, teach them to multiply using their fingers, as follows:

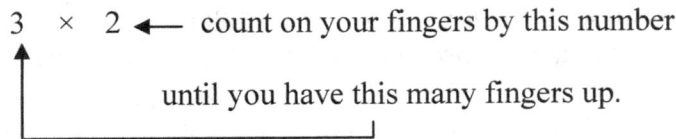

3×2 ← count on your fingers by this number

until you have this many fingers up.

The number you reach is the answer.

Give your student practice with questions like:

$4 \times 5 = \rule{1cm}{0.15mm}$ $3 \times 3 = \rule{1cm}{0.15mm}$ $5 \times 2 = \rule{1cm}{0.15mm}$

$2 \times 3 = \rule{1cm}{0.15mm}$ $3 \times 5 = \rule{1cm}{0.15mm}$ $4 \times 5 = \rule{1cm}{0.15mm}$

Point out that 2×3 means: add three, two times (that's what you are doing as you count up on your fingers). Don't belabour this point though — you can always explain it in more depth when your student is further into the unit.

Your student should be able to count and multiply with ease by twos, threes and fives on one hand before you teach the next section. As it is important to create a sense of momentum in your lessons (while still teaching by steps and allowing lots of repetition), you shouldn't expect a more delayed student to learn any table other than the fours (on one hand) as you progress through the rest of the unit. After your student has written the Confidence Building Unit Test you can introduce higher tables. (With a more motivated or knowledgeable student, you can demand more: you might draw a new hand on their homework every few weeks and ask them to memorize it. You might also assign questions where they are required to use higher tables.)

IMPORTANT NOTE: Do not move on until <u>all</u> of your students have gotten 100% on the diagnostic quiz (Question 4) on worksheet F-1 (continued). Also make sure your students can add and subtract one digit numbers as taught in the Appendix. Students can learn the skills required to do well in this unit very quickly—**do not move on until you have taught the skills covered in this section.**
Any time you see a stop sign (⬡), it is a signal for you to stop and verify that all your students have grasped the skill before you move on.

Section F-2: Naming Fractions

Explain how to represent a fraction.

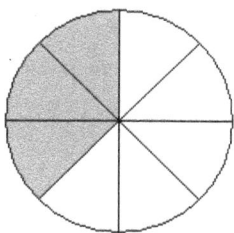

$$\frac{3}{8}$$ ← Step 1: Count the number of shaded regions
← Step 2: Count the number of pieces the pie is cut into

Remember, each step should be taught separately (allowing for repetition) unless your student is very quick.

Here are some questions your student can try.

What fraction of each figure is shaded?

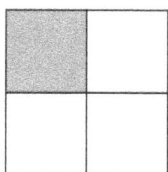

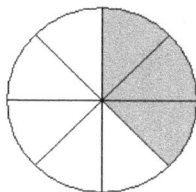

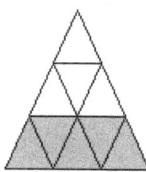

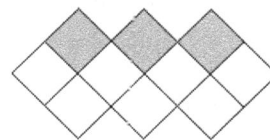

Teach your student how to draw $\frac{1}{2}$ and $\frac{1}{4}$ with circles.

Teach them how to draw $\frac{1}{3}$ as follows:

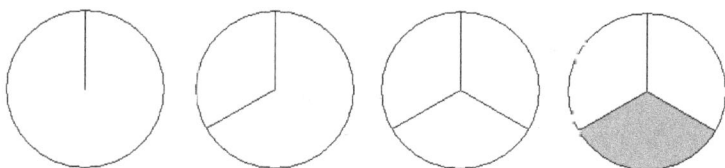

Ask your student how they would draw $\frac{1}{2}$ and $\frac{1}{4}$ in a square box. Make sure they know that in drawing a fraction, you have to make all the pieces the same size. For instance, the following is **not** a good example of $\frac{1}{4}$:

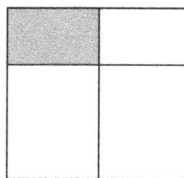

Your student should be able to recognize when a shaded piece of pie is less than $\frac{1}{2}$ of a pie.

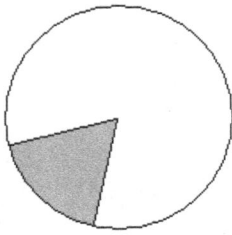

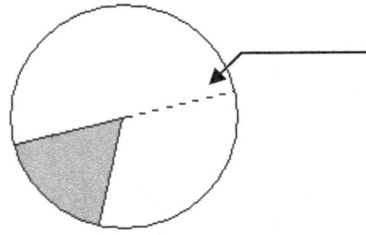

To see that the fraction is less than $\frac{1}{2}$, continue one of the lines.

NOTE TO THE CLASSROOM TEACHER: If some of your students finish worksheet F-2 early, ask them to draw a circle on the worksheet (wherever they can find room) and draw a picture of $\frac{1}{4}$. Then if they need more work, ask them to draw $\frac{3}{4}, \frac{1}{3}, \frac{2}{3}, \frac{1}{8}, \frac{5}{8}$, etc. You can ask students to draw a pie, cut it into thirds, then cut each piece in two to show sixths. Then students can draw $\frac{1}{6}, \frac{5}{6}$, etc. To buy time, you can also ask students if they can figure out how to draw twelfths and sixteenths. As you assign progressively harder questions, make a big deal about how well your students are doing.

Section F-3: Adding Two Fractions With the Same Denominator
Rule: Add the numerator and leave the denominator the same.

For example,

$$\frac{1}{4} \quad + \quad \frac{2}{4} \quad = \quad \frac{3}{4}$$

1 piece plus 2 pieces gives 3 pieces

Make sure your student knows why the denominator does not change: the pie is still cut into 4 pieces—you are still adding up $\frac{1}{4}$ size pieces.

Allow for lots of practice. Only introduce one step at a time.

Whenever possible, you should allow the student to figure out how to extend a concept to a case they haven't seen. This is easy to do with the addition of fractions. Ask your student what they might do if:

There were three fractions with the same denominator?

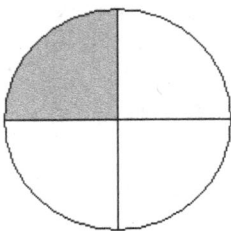

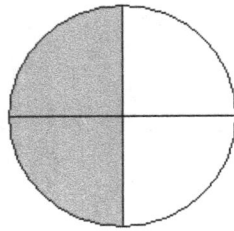

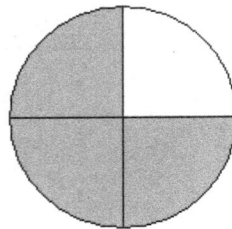

$$\frac{1}{7} + \frac{2}{7} + \frac{4}{7} = ?$$

(If your student guesses what to do in this case, point out that they are smart enough to figure out mathematical rules by themselves. It is essential that you make your student feel intelligent and capable right from the first lesson.)

If they had subtraction?

$$\frac{3}{4} - \frac{1}{4} = ?$$

Demonstrate this with a picture:

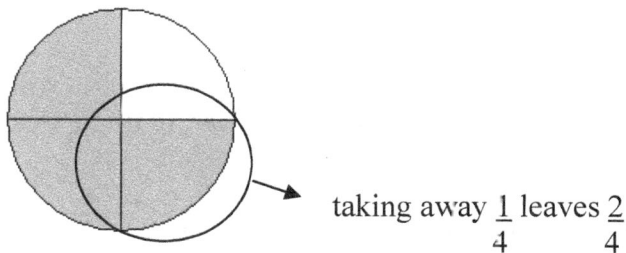

taking away $\frac{1}{4}$ leaves $\frac{2}{4}$

If they had mixed addition and subtraction?

$$\frac{5}{7} + \frac{1}{7} - \frac{3}{7} = ?$$

NOTE TO THE CLASSROOM TEACHER: Let students know how impressed you are when they answer the ADVANCED and BONUS questions on worksheet F3-A. When you hand out the worksheet to the class, you can say to the class: "There's a very tricky question at the bottom of the page – the bonus question – so watch out." Students are always thrilled at not falling for the trick. When a student has completed worksheet F3-A, you can ask: "Do you think you can handle a question with four fractions?" Then write $\frac{1}{17} + \frac{1}{17} + \frac{1}{17} + \frac{1}{17}$ (or a harder question) across the bottom of their page. Students generally respond to this approach and are excited about meeting the challenge.

Section F-4: Adding Fractions With Different Denominators

If the denominators are different, then you can't compare piece sizes — it's not clear how to add fractions with different denominators.

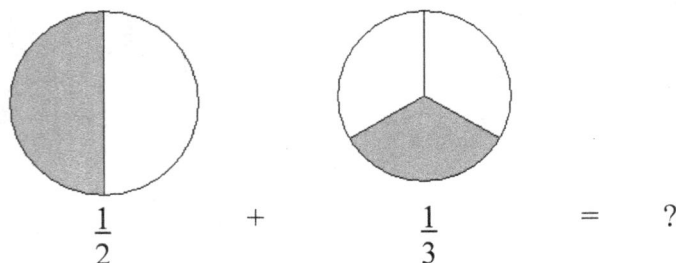

$$\frac{1}{2} \quad + \quad \frac{1}{3} \quad = \quad ?$$

Tell your student that after you have shown them how the operation works with pictures you will show them a much easier method that they cannot fail to perform. (You should, however, return to this sort of pictorial explanation when your student has fully mastered the operation).

Solution: Cut each of the two pieces in the first pie into three, and cut each of the three pieces in the second pie into two. This will give the same number of pieces in each because $2 \times 3 = 3 \times 2 = 6$

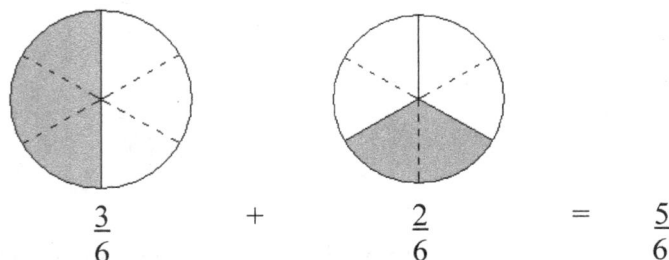

$$\frac{3}{6} \quad + \quad \frac{2}{6} \quad = \quad \frac{5}{6}$$

Draw the above picture, and ask your student to write the new fractions corresponding to the way pies are now cut. Make sure they notice that $\frac{1}{2}$ is the same as $\frac{3}{6}$ of the pie, and that $\frac{1}{3}$ is the same as $\frac{2}{6}$ (and one out of three pieces is the same as two out of six). Once you have discussed this, your student can perform the addition. The one thing the student should take away from this explanation is that to produce pieces of the same size in both pies (which is necessary for adding fractions), one has to cut each pie into smaller pieces. (For more advanced students: the number of pieces you need to cut both pies into is equal to the lowest common multiple of the denominators — see Section F-9).

Tell your student you will now teach them a very easy way of changing the number of pieces the pie is cut into without having to draw the picture.

Step 1: Multiply each denominator by the other one. The numerator also has to be multiplied, because now you are getting more pieces:

$$\frac{3 \times 1}{3 \times 2} + \frac{1 \times 2}{3 \times 2}$$

Have your student practise this step before you go on. The student should just practise setting the right numbers in the right places. Remember you can make this step easier if necessary by having the student move one denominator at a time.

Step 2: Perform the multiplication.

$$\frac{3}{3} \times \frac{1}{2} + \frac{1}{3} \times \frac{2}{2} = \frac{3}{6} + \frac{2}{6}$$

Practise Step 1, then Step 1 and Step 2 together, before you go on.

Step 3: Perform the addition.

$$\frac{3}{6} + \frac{2}{6} = \frac{5}{6}$$

Now have the student practise all three steps.

For students who know higher times tables, gradually mix in higher denominators like 6 and 7 (make sure the smaller denominator does not divide the larger).

NOTE: Two numbers are relatively prime if their least-common multiple (the lowest number they both divide into evenly) is their product. For instance, 2 and 3 are relatively prime but 4 and 6 are not (since the product of 4 and 6 is 24, while their least common multiple is 12). The method of adding fractions taught in this section is only really efficient for fractions whose denominators are relatively prime (as is the case for all of the examples directly above). For other cases, for instance when one denominator divides into the other or when both denominators divide into a number that is smaller than their product, more efficient methods can be found in sections F-5 and F-9.

Section F-5: Changing One Denominator
Tell your student that sometimes you don't have to change both denominators (i.e. there's a short-cut) when you add fractions. How can you tell when you can do less work?

Step 1: Check to see if the smaller denominator divides into the larger. Count up on your fingers by the smaller denominator and see if you hit the larger denominator — if you do, the number of fingers you have up is what you multiply the smaller denominator by:

$$\frac{1}{2} + \frac{1}{10} = \frac{5 \times 1}{5 \times 2} + \frac{1}{10}$$

Counting up by twos you hit 10. You have 5 fingers up. This means $5 \times 2 = 10$

Multiply the smaller denominator by the number of fingers you have up

Give lots of practice at this step before you move on.

jump math
MULTIPLYING POTENTIAL.

Step 2: Perform the multiplication.

$$\frac{5 \times 1}{5 \times 2} + \frac{1}{10} = \frac{5}{10} + \frac{1}{10}$$

Step 3: Perform the addition.

$$\frac{5}{10} + \frac{1}{10} = \frac{6}{10}$$

Extra: Ask your student how they would do

$$\frac{1}{2} - \frac{1}{10} =$$

Here are some sample questions you can use during this lesson:

(1) $\frac{1}{2} + \frac{1}{10}$ (2) $\frac{3}{4} + \frac{1}{8}$ (3) $\frac{1}{5} + \frac{1}{10}$ (4) $\frac{1}{8} + \frac{1}{2}$

(5) $\frac{1}{3} + \frac{1}{6}$ (6) $\frac{1}{4} + \frac{1}{12}$ (7) $\frac{2}{3} + \frac{1}{15}$ (8) $\frac{1}{5} + \frac{1}{20}$

(9) $\frac{7}{25} + \frac{2}{5}$ (10) $\frac{1}{2} - \frac{1}{4}$ (11) $\frac{2}{3} - \frac{1}{9}$ (12) $\frac{7}{15} - \frac{1}{3}$

NOTE: If you think your student might have trouble with this section, you should start with the following exercise: tell your student that the number 2 "goes into" or "divides" the numbers they say when they are counting up by twos (i.e., 2 divides 2, 4, 6, 8, 10, etc.). Write several numbers between 2 and 10 in a column and ask your student to write "yes" beside the numbers that 2 goes into, and "no" beside the others. When your student has mastered this step, repeat the exercise with numbers between 3 and 15 (for counting by threes) and numbers between 5 and 25 divisible by 5 (for counting by fives). Tell your student that when they are adding fractions, they should always check to see if the smaller denominator divides into the larger; when this is the case they only have to change the smaller denominator.

Section F-6: Distinguishing Among the Three Methods Taught Thus Far
This is an important section. For many students, it may be the first time they are taught how to decide which of several algorithms they should use to perform an operation.

Step 1: As a warm-up exercise, write a number on the board. Have your student tell you whether they say that number while counting by 2. Repeat the exercise but counting by 3's and then by 5's.

Do not move on until <u>all</u> of your students have gotten 100% on the diagnostic quiz (Questions 1, 2, & 3 on worksheet F-6 A).

Step 2: Identify the lesser denominator.

Step 3: Count up by that number and see if you hit the greater denominator (i.e. see if the lesser divides or goes into the greater evenly). If yes, write "yes." If not, write "no." In other words, the student is identifying whether or not they will have to change one fraction (short-cut) or both fractions (no short-cut) before adding.

Practise these steps on a variety of different pairs of fractions before going on.

Note on F-6 B, Question 2: If the student has written "same," add the fractions using the procedure in F-3. If they have written "no" then follow the procedure in Section F-4, and if they have written "yes" then follow the procedure in F-5.

Typical Exercise:
(1) $\dfrac{1}{7} + \dfrac{2}{7}$
(2) $\dfrac{3}{5} + \dfrac{1}{15}$
(3) $\dfrac{3}{4} + \dfrac{1}{5}$

Section F-7: Adding Three Fractions
Let your student know that this is an enriched unit. Adding triple fractions is normally not covered until Grade 6 or 7.

Give questions where two smaller denominators go into the larger, i.e.

$$\dfrac{1}{2} + \dfrac{1}{3} + \dfrac{1}{6}$$

$$\dfrac{3 \times 1}{3 \times 2} + \dfrac{1 \times 2}{3 \times 2} + \dfrac{1}{6}$$

$$\dfrac{3}{6} + \dfrac{2}{6} + \dfrac{1}{6} = \dfrac{6}{6}$$

Note: When you first teach this section, always place the fractions with the two lowest denominators first. After your student has mastered this, you can change the order and ask them to identify which denominators have to be changed.

Here are some sample questions you can use during this lesson:

(1) $\dfrac{1}{2} + \dfrac{1}{3} + \dfrac{1}{6}$
(2) $\dfrac{2}{3} + \dfrac{1}{5} + \dfrac{1}{15}$
(3) $\dfrac{3}{4} + \dfrac{1}{2} + \dfrac{1}{8}$

Section F-8: Equivalent Fractions and Reducing Fractions

First check to see if your student knows how to divide by a single-digit number. If not, teach them as follows: $15 \div 3 = ?$

Count up by the number that comes after the division sign, until you reach the number in front of the sign; the number of fingers you have up is the answer; i.e. 3 divides 15 five times, because it takes five 3s to add up to 15. Give lots of practice. Then explain to your student that the same fraction can have different representations:

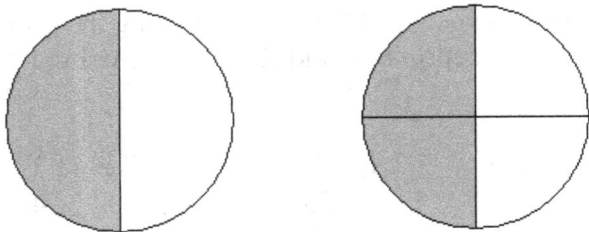

For instance, with $\frac{1}{2}$ of a pie and $\frac{2}{4}$ of a pie you get the same amount of pie.

Each fraction has a representation in the smallest possible whole numbers. Finding this representation is called reducing the fraction.

To check whether a fraction can be represented with smaller numbers, your student should first check if the numerator divides into the denominator.

Step 1: $\frac{5}{15}$ Count up by the numerator to see if it divides into the denominator

Step 2:   If yes, divide both the numerator and the denominator of the fraction by the numerator:

$$\frac{5 \div 5}{15 \div 5} = \frac{1}{3}$$

Some students will need a good deal of practice with step 1. You might give your student a sheet of questions on which they simply have to count up by the numerator, checking to see if they say the denominator as they count.

Once your student has mastered the steps above, let them know that if the numerator of a fraction does not divide the denominator, they should still check to see if any smaller number divides both. If they find a number that goes into the numerator and the denominator, they should reduce the fraction as follows:

$$\frac{4 \div 2}{6 \div 2} = \frac{2}{3}$$

You might start by giving your student hints. You might say, for instance, "The numerator and denominator of this fraction either divide by 2 or by 3. Check which one works."

Here are some sample questions you can use during this lesson:

Division:

$25 \div 5 =$ ___ $\qquad$ $16 \div 4 =$ ___ $\qquad$ $8 \div 2 =$ ___ $\qquad$ $12 \div 3 =$ ___

$15 \div 5 =$ ___ $\qquad$ $6 \div 2 =$ ___ $\qquad$ $10 \div 2 =$ ___ $\qquad$ $20 \div 4 =$ ___

Reducing fractions (easier):

$\dfrac{5}{15} =$ $\qquad$ $\dfrac{2}{8} =$ $\qquad$ $\dfrac{2}{6} =$ $\qquad$ $\dfrac{3}{6} =$ $\qquad$ $\dfrac{3}{9} =$ $\qquad$ $\dfrac{5}{25} =$

Reducing fractions (harder):

$\dfrac{4}{6} =$ $\qquad$ $\dfrac{6}{8} =$ $\qquad$ $\dfrac{8}{10} =$ $\qquad$ $\dfrac{8}{12} =$ $\qquad$ $\dfrac{6}{9} =$ $\qquad$ $\dfrac{9}{15} =$

NOTE: If your student has just learned to multiply, only ask them to reduce fractions where the numerator and denominator divide by 2, 3 or 5. You should give them the same questions repeatedly for homework as it may take them some time to get used to reducing.

Section F-9: Finding the Lowest Common Denominator
(This section should only be taught to second year JUMP students or to very advanced first years.)

The lowest common multiple (LCM) of two numbers is the lowest number that both divide into evenly. For instance, the lowest common multiple of 4 and 6 is 12. Notice that the lowest common multiple of 4 and 6 *is lower than* their product ($4 \times 6 = 24$). But with other numbers, say 2 and 3, the lowest common multiple *is* the product. To find the lowest common multiple of a pair of numbers, simply count up by the larger number and keep checking if the smaller divides into the result.

Example: 4 and 6.
　　Count up by sixes.
　　6　　　　4 does not go into 6. Keep counting up.
　　12　　　4 goes into 12.
　　Therefore, LCM = 12

Example: 2 and 3.
　　Count up by threes.
　　3　　　　2 does not go into 3. Keep counting up.
　　6　　　　2 goes into 6.
　　Therefore, LCM = 6

Example: 2 and 10.
　　Count up by tens.
　　10　　　2 goes into 10.
　　Therefore, LCM = 10

By counting up, have your student find the LCM of the following pairs. Also have them say whether the LCM is equal to the product, or less than the product.

3 and 5	2 and 8	4 and 6
4 and 10	5 and 10	6 and 9
2 and 10	5 and 4	3 and 4
6 and 8	8 and 10	2 and 7

The method of adding fractions we taught in sections F-4 to F-6 doesn't always yield a final denominator that is the LCM of the two denominators; by our method the student would add $\frac{1}{4}$ and $\frac{1}{6}$ by changing both fractions as follows:

$$\frac{1}{4} + \frac{1}{6} \longrightarrow \frac{6}{6} \times \frac{1}{4} + \frac{1}{6} \times \frac{4}{4} \longrightarrow \frac{6}{24} + \frac{4}{24} \longrightarrow \frac{10}{24}$$

$\frac{10}{24}$ can be reduced (see Section F-8) to $\frac{5}{12}$

If the student thinks that the LCM of a pair of denominators may be lower than the product, then (to avoid having to reduce the answer) they should proceed as follows:

To find the LCM, count up by the larger denominator (in this case 6) until you reach a number that the smaller denominator divides into. Counting by sixes you get 12, and you can stop counting there because 4 divides into 12, so the student can use 12 as the denominator:

$$\frac{1}{4} + \frac{1}{6} \longrightarrow \frac{3}{3} \times \frac{1}{4} + \frac{1}{6} \times \frac{2}{2} \longrightarrow \frac{3}{12} + \frac{2}{12} \longrightarrow \frac{5}{12}$$

Make sure your student knows the LCM is also called the lowest common denominator.

Your student should try these questions:

$$\frac{1}{6} + \frac{3}{8} \qquad \frac{1}{6} + \frac{1}{10} \qquad \frac{3}{8} + \frac{5}{12}$$

This method will also work for triple fractions:

$$\frac{1}{5} + \frac{1}{6} + \frac{1}{10}$$

Tell the student to count up by the larger denominator, and at each stage check if the smaller denominators divide the number you have reached. For instance: two 10s are 20, but 6 does not divide 20, so the student should keep counting by tens. Three 10s are 30, and 5 and 6 both divide 30, so the student should use 30 as the denominator.

Here are some sample (Grade 8 level) questions you can use during this lesson:

(1) $\dfrac{1}{4} + \dfrac{1}{3} + \dfrac{1}{6}$ (2) $\dfrac{1}{4} + \dfrac{1}{6} + \dfrac{1}{8}$ (3) $\dfrac{3}{5} + \dfrac{1}{6} + \dfrac{7}{10}$

Section F-10: Mixed Fractions and Improper Fractions

If the numerator of a fraction is bigger than the denominator, the fraction is called an improper fraction. Any improper fraction can also be written as a mixed fraction, that is, as a combination of a whole number and a fraction. For instance:

$$\frac{3}{2} = 1\frac{1}{2}$$

You can explain these two ways of writing a fraction with a picture.

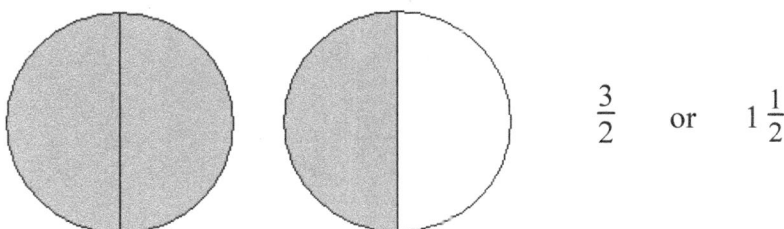

$\dfrac{3}{2}$ or $1\dfrac{1}{2}$

Three half-size pieces of a pie are the same as one whole pie, plus an extra half.

How to write a fraction as an improper fraction:

Example:

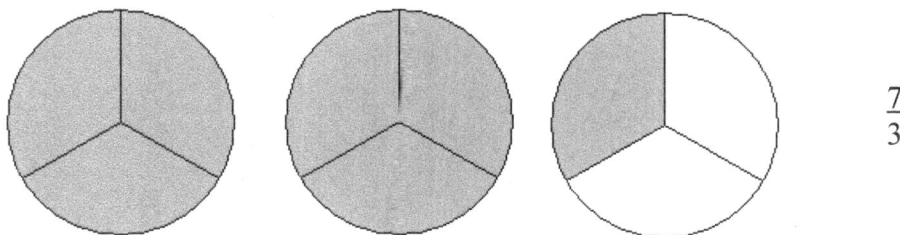

$\dfrac{7}{3}$

Step 1: How many pieces are shaded? Answer: 7. Put this number in the numerator.

Step 2: How many pieces is each pie cut into? Answer: 3. Put this number in the denominator. (Even though you have more than one pie, the piece size doesn't change – you still have third-size pieces in each pie – 7 altogether.)

How to write a fraction as a mixed fraction:

Example:

$2\frac{1}{3}$

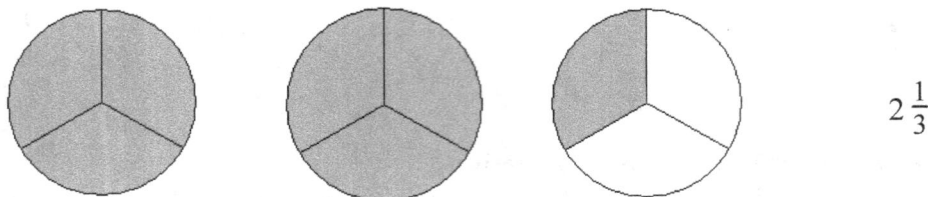

Step 1: How many whole pies are there? Answer: 2. Write this down as a whole number.

Step 2: Write down what fraction of a pie you have in the last pie.

Give your student lots of practice in the two ways of writing a fraction. Here are some examples you might use:

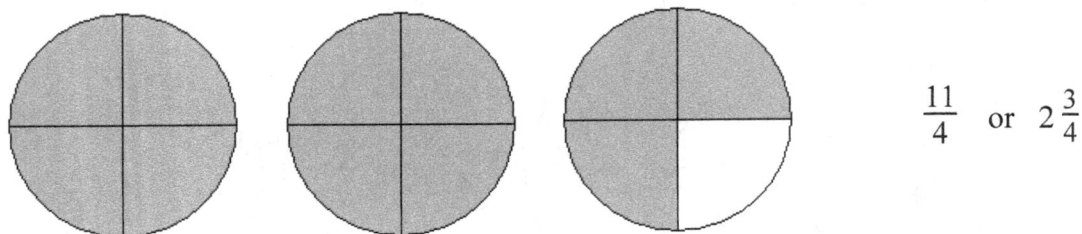

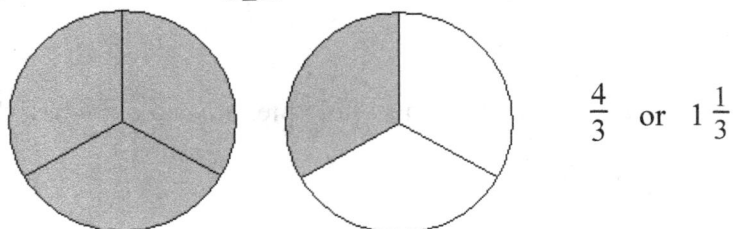

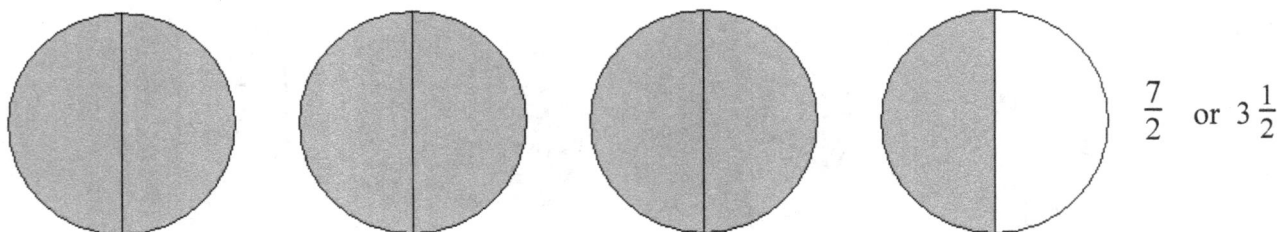

$\frac{11}{4}$ or $2\frac{3}{4}$

$\frac{4}{3}$ or $1\frac{1}{3}$

$\frac{7}{2}$ or $3\frac{1}{2}$

Your student should be able to draw simple, mixed fractions like $1\frac{1}{2}, 2\frac{1}{2}, 1\frac{1}{3}, 2\frac{1}{3}, 1\frac{1}{4}, 1\frac{3}{4}$.

Your student should also be able to decide, in simple cases, which of two mixed fractions is larger. For instance:

$2\frac{1}{2}$ or $3\frac{1}{2}$ $1\frac{1}{4}$ or $2\frac{5}{6}$ $1\frac{1}{3}$ or $1\frac{1}{4}$

Your student should be able to explain how they can tell when a fraction represents more than a whole pie: i.e. they should be able to say "when the top (or numerator) is larger than the bottom (or denominator) you have more than one pie."

As a test, write out several fractions and ask your student to identify the fractions that represent more than one whole pie. For instance,

$$\frac{5}{6} \qquad \frac{7}{4} \qquad \frac{2}{3} \qquad \frac{12}{5}$$

IMPORTANT NOTE: GRADE 3 & 4 TEACHERS STOP HERE!!

If you are a **Grade 3-4 classroom teacher** participating in the JUMP In-Class program, you are only expected to teach up to section F-10. When you are sure your students understand the material in Sections F-1 to F10 you can give them the Practice Test – Level C, and then the Final Test – Level C.

Grade 5 & 6 teachers should complete the entire unit and then give the Practice and Final Tests – Level D. (All tests are included at the end of this Manual.)

Section F-11: Converting Fractions (Without Pictures)

Converting Mixed Fractions into Improper Fractions:

Example: Step ②: 6 + 1 = 7

$$2\frac{1}{3} \;=\; \frac{7}{3} \impliedby \text{Step ③}$$

Step ①   ×

Step 1: Multiply the whole number by the denominator (i.e. $2 \times 3 = 6$). To explain this step, point out that in the two whole pies (each cut into three pieces), there are six pieces.

Step 2: Add the number you got in the last step to the numerator. Put the sum in the numerator of your improper fraction. (To explain this step, point out that in the one-third pie you have one piece which has to be added to the six pieces in the two whole pies, giving seven pieces altogether.)

Step 3: Write the denominator of the mixed fraction in the denominator of the improper fraction. (The two fractions have the same denominator because the piece size is still one-third.)

Here are some sample questions you can use during this lesson:

$$2\frac{1}{2} = \qquad 3\frac{1}{3} = \qquad 5\frac{1}{2} = \qquad 4\frac{1}{3} = \qquad 3\frac{2}{3} = \qquad 1\frac{1}{3} =$$

$$4\frac{1}{5} = \qquad 3\frac{4}{5} = \qquad 5\frac{2}{5} = \qquad 5\frac{2}{3} = \qquad 4\frac{3}{4} = \qquad 5\frac{1}{6} =$$

Section F-12: Converting Fractions

Converting Improper Fractions into Mixed Fractions:

First, you may have to teach your student how to divide when the divisor doesn't go evenly into the number being divided:

Example: $2 \overline{\smash)9}$

Step 1: Count up on your fingers by the divisor (i.e., 2) until you reach a number just below the number being divided (i.e., 9).

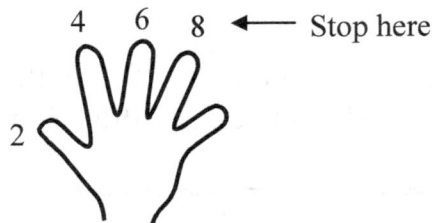

4   6   8 ← Stop here

2

If the student has trouble knowing when they should stop counting up, practise this step with various examples:

$$2 \overline{\smash)11} \qquad\qquad 3 \overline{\smash)10} \qquad\qquad 5 \overline{\smash)17}$$

If your student is really struggling with this step, write the numbers from 1 to 10 and circle the numbers divisible by 2. This will help your student see when to stop counting. Repeat this with the numbers between 1 and 15 (for counting by threes) and 1 and 25 (for counting by fives).

Step 2: Write the number of fingers you have up on top of the division sign:

$$2 \overline{\smash)9\,}^{\;4}$$

Step 3: Write the number you reached on your fingers below the number being divided:

$$2 \overline{\smash)9\,}^{\;4}$$
$$\phantom{2 \overline{\smash)}}8$$

<u>Step 4:</u> Subtract to find the remainder:

$$2 \overline{\smash{\big)}\ 9} \quad \begin{array}{r} 4 \\ -8 \\ \hline 1 \end{array} \qquad\qquad 2 \overline{\smash{\big)}\ 9} \quad \begin{array}{r} 4\ \text{R}\ 1 \\ -8 \\ \hline 1 \end{array}$$

Explain that the answer on top means that 2 fits into 9 four times with 1 left over. You might draw a picture to illustrate this:

 ◁—————— remainder 1

How to convert an improper fraction into a mixed fraction:

<u>Step 1:</u> Rewrite the fraction as a division statement: $\dfrac{9}{2} \longrightarrow 2 \overline{\smash{\big)}\ 9}$

Have the student practise putting the right number in the right place.

<u>Step 2:</u> Do the long division. Your student should know how to do this from the previous section:

$$2 \overline{\smash{\big)}\ 9} \quad \begin{array}{r} 4\ \text{R}\ 1 \\ -8 \\ \hline 1 \end{array}$$

<u>Step 3:</u> Use the answer to the division problem to write the mixed fraction:

$$\dfrac{9}{2} = 4\tfrac{1}{2} \qquad\qquad 2 \overline{\smash{\big)}\ 9} \quad \begin{array}{r} 4\ \text{R}\ 1 \\ -8 \\ \hline 1 \end{array}$$

After your student has learned to convert improper fractions to mixed fractions, teach them to estimate how many whole pies an improper fraction represents. For instance $\dfrac{7}{3}$ is at least two whole pies because 3 divides into 7 two times (the remainder, 1, is the number of fractional pieces in the last pie plate).

Your student should be able to say, in simple cases, which of two improper fractions is larger. For instance, $\dfrac{7}{2}$ is larger than $\dfrac{11}{5}$ because in the first case you have at least three whole pies, and in the latter, two.

They should also be able to say when an improper fraction is bigger than a whole number. For instance, $\dfrac{7}{3}$ is bigger than 2.

Finally, your student should know that an improper fraction is always bigger than a proper fraction. You might write out several pairs and have them identify the larger; for instance, $^5/_6$ and $^7/_5$.

Here are some sample questions you can use during this lesson:

$$\frac{5}{2} = \qquad \frac{7}{2} = \qquad \frac{7}{3} = \qquad \frac{9}{2} = \qquad \frac{11}{3} = \qquad \frac{9}{4} =$$

$$\frac{16}{5} = \qquad \frac{12}{5} = \qquad \frac{23}{5} = \qquad \frac{17}{4} = \qquad \frac{11}{2} = \qquad \frac{17}{5} =$$

NOTE: Maggie Licata (JUMP's former Executive Director) suggested a method for converting improper fractions to mixed fractions which might be easier than the one given above (her method also enables students to do the conversions in their heads). If you use the following method, you should still, at some point, teach your student how to do long division by the method above.

Change $\frac{9}{2}$ to a mixed fraction:

Step 1: Count by the denominator until you reach a number just below the number being divided. (This is just step 1, as outlined above)

Step 2: Write the number of fingers you have raised (i.e. four fingers) as a whole number:

$$\frac{9}{2} = \quad 4$$

NOTE TO THE CLASSROOM TEACHER: Before you proceed, you should give students a diagnostic test on identifying how many whole pies there are in an improper fraction:

$$\text{i.e.,} \quad \frac{11}{5} = 2 \text{ whole pies (+ 1 piece left over)} \qquad \frac{14}{4} = 3 \text{ whole pies (+ 2 pieces left over)}$$

(Make it clear to students that the remainder in the division statements is the number of pieces left over.)

Step 3: Write the numerator of the original fraction beside the whole number:

$$\frac{9}{2} = \quad 4 \, \frac{}{2}$$

Step 4: Multiply the whole number by the denominator:

$$2 \times 4 = 8$$

Step 5: Subtract the result of step 4 from the denominator of the improper fraction:

$$9 - 8 = 1$$

<u>Step 6:</u> The answer from step 5 is the numerator of the mixed fraction:

$$\frac{9}{2} \; = \; 4\frac{1}{2}$$

If your student has trouble with step 5, teach them to subtract as follows (see also the Appendix):

$$17 - 15 = ?$$

<u>Step 1:</u> Say the second number ("15") with your fist closed.

<u>Step 2:</u> Raising one finger at a time, count until you reach the first number (i.e. the student raises one finger when they say "16" and another when they say "17"). The number of fingers you have up is the answer. Give your student lots of practice at this. (Eventually you can use fairly large numbers like 178 – 173 to boost your student's confidence. Make sure the numbers you pick aren't too widely separated: for numbers that have a difference greater than 10, it is better to subtract by lining the numbers up in the traditional way.)

Section F-13: Adding Mixed Fractions
Converting fractions to improper fractions, then adding them.

Example: $1\frac{1}{2} \; + \; 2\frac{1}{4}$

First, convert the fractions to improper fractions (see Section F-10):

$$1\frac{1}{2} \; + \; 2\frac{1}{4} \; = \; \frac{3}{2} \; + \; \frac{9}{4}$$

Now add the fractions (as taught in F-4 to F-5):

$$1\frac{1}{2} \; + \; 2\frac{1}{4} \; = \; \frac{3}{2} \; + \; \frac{9}{4} \; = \; \frac{2 \times 3}{2 \times 2} \; + \; \frac{9}{4} \; = \; \frac{6}{2} \; + \; \frac{9}{4} \; = \; \frac{15}{4}$$

Here are some sample questions you can use during this lesson:

$$1\frac{1}{2} + 2\frac{1}{3} = \qquad 2\frac{1}{2} + 1\frac{1}{3} = \qquad \frac{1}{2} + 1\frac{1}{5} = \qquad 2\frac{2}{3} + 3\frac{1}{4} =$$

$$2\frac{1}{2} + 1\frac{3}{4} = \qquad 3\frac{1}{2} + 5\frac{1}{4} = \qquad \frac{2}{5} + 1\frac{1}{2} = \qquad \frac{3}{4} + 2\frac{1}{5} =$$

NOTE: There is a method of adding fractions that is more efficient than the one taught above when the whole numbers or the denominators of the fractions are large. If your student finds fractions easy, you might teach them the following method (otherwise wait until your student has completed several other units of the manual).

Add:
$$8\frac{1}{2} + 5\frac{1}{3}$$

Step 1: Make the denominators of the fractions the same (as you would if you were simply adding the fractions):

$$8\frac{1}{2} + 5\frac{1}{3} \longrightarrow 8\frac{1 \times 3}{2 \times 3} + 5\frac{1 \times 2}{3 \times 2} \longrightarrow 8\frac{3}{6} + 5\frac{2}{6}$$

Step 2: Add the whole numbers (8 and 5) and the fractions ($\frac{3}{6}$ and $\frac{2}{6}$) separately, but write your answer as a single mixed fraction:

$$8\frac{3}{6} + 5\frac{2}{6} \longrightarrow 13\frac{5}{6}$$

In some cases, the fractional part of the answer may be an improper fraction. For instance:

$$8\frac{1}{2} + 5\frac{2}{3} \longrightarrow 8\frac{1 \times 3}{2 \times 3} + 5\frac{2 \times 2}{3 \times 2} \longrightarrow 8\frac{3}{6} + 5\frac{4}{6} \longrightarrow 13\frac{7}{6}$$

In this case, your student should change their answer as follows:

Step 1: Rewrite your answer as the sum of a whole number and a fraction:

$$13\frac{7}{6} = 13 + \frac{7}{6}$$

Step 2: Rewrite the improper fraction as a mixed fraction (as taught in Section F-12):

$$13 + \frac{7}{6} = 13 + 1\frac{1}{6}$$

Step 3: Add:

$$13 + 1\frac{1}{6} = 14\frac{1}{6}$$

Section F-14: Comparing Fractions
First teach your student the meaning of the "greater than"(>) and "less than"(<) signs. Tell them the arrow should always point from the larger number to the smaller number.

Example:
$$2 > 1 \quad \text{"Two is greater than one."}$$
$$2 < 3 \quad \text{"Two is less than three"}$$

Give the student practice filling in the sign with whole numbers.

Example:

$$7 \; ? \; 9 \longrightarrow 7 < 9$$

Now, tell your student that to compare the size of two fractions you simply have to convert the fractions to the same denominator. The fraction with the larger numerator is the larger fraction.

Example:

$$\frac{2}{3} \; ? \; \frac{5}{6} \longrightarrow \frac{2 \times 2}{2 \times 3} \; ? \; \frac{5}{6} \longrightarrow \frac{4}{6} < \frac{5}{6}$$

Note: If you would prefer not to teach your student about inequalities at this stage, you could simply ask them to circle the bigger fraction.

Section F-15: Word Problems

Here are some word problems from a Grade 7 book you could try:

1. Ken ate $\frac{5}{8}$ of a pizza and Nola ate $\frac{1}{4}$. What fraction of the pizza was eaten?

2. On Monday Mike ran for $\frac{1}{4}$ hour in the morning and $\frac{1}{2}$ hour in the afternoon. What fraction of an hour did Mike run on Monday?

3. Over one supper hour Carl used $\frac{1}{2}$ of a container of tomatoes, and $\frac{1}{6}$ of a container of olives. How many containers of toppings did he use?

Give your students other questions of this sort.

NOTE: Your student may now write the Fraction Test. Please use the Practice Test – Level D (pages 42-43) first. Once you have identified and reviewed any weaker areas, and are sure that your student is prepared and confident, follow up with the Final Test – Level D (pages 44-45). The Practice and Final Tests – Level C are intended for students in Grades 3 or 4.

If your student scores 80% or higher, they can move on. If they don't score 80% or higher, review the material they had trouble with and let them write the test again. (Make sure you let your student know, before you give them the test, that they can write it as many times as they need to.) Let your student know that the material in the test goes up to a Grade 6/7 level.

F-3 HW:
Adding and Subtracting Fractions

1. Name these fractions.

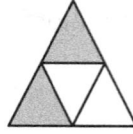

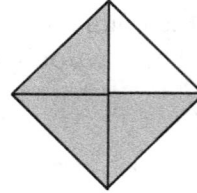

2. Add.

a) $\dfrac{1}{3} + \dfrac{1}{3}$

b) $\dfrac{2}{7} + \dfrac{3}{7}$

c) $\dfrac{2}{11} + \dfrac{1}{11}$

d) $\dfrac{1}{20} + \dfrac{10}{20}$

e) $\dfrac{2}{6} + \dfrac{3}{6}$

f) $\dfrac{1}{15} + \dfrac{2}{15} + \dfrac{5}{15}$

3. Subtract.

a) $\dfrac{4}{4} - \dfrac{1}{4}$

b) $\dfrac{4}{8} - \dfrac{3}{8}$

c) $\dfrac{6}{7} - \dfrac{1}{7}$

BONUS: $\dfrac{2}{11} + \dfrac{5}{11} - \dfrac{3}{11}$

F-4 HW:
Adding and Subtracting Fractions

1. Name these fractions.

a)

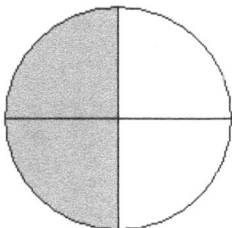

b)

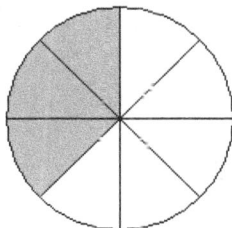

c)

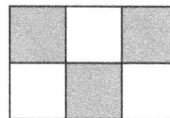

2. Add or subtract.

a) $\dfrac{1}{3} + \dfrac{1}{3}$

b) $\dfrac{2}{7} + \dfrac{3}{7}$

c) $\dfrac{1}{15} + \dfrac{2}{15} + \dfrac{5}{15}$

d) $\dfrac{3}{7} - \dfrac{1}{7}$

e) $\dfrac{9}{11} - \dfrac{2}{11}$

f) $\dfrac{3}{9} + \dfrac{4}{9} - \dfrac{2}{9}$

3. Add or Subtract

a) $\dfrac{1}{2} + \dfrac{1}{3}$

b) $\dfrac{1}{3} + \dfrac{1}{5}$

c) $\dfrac{1}{2} + \dfrac{1}{5}$

d) $\dfrac{3}{5} + \dfrac{1}{2}$

e) $\dfrac{4}{5} + \dfrac{1}{2}$

f) $\dfrac{1}{5} + \dfrac{2}{3}$

g) $\dfrac{2}{3} - \dfrac{1}{2}$

h) $\dfrac{1}{2} - \dfrac{1}{3}$

I) $\dfrac{3}{5} - \dfrac{1}{2}$

F-5 HW:
Adding and Subtracting Fractions

1. Add or subtract (*don't* change the denominators).

a) $\dfrac{1}{5} + \dfrac{3}{5}$

b) $\dfrac{2}{7} + \dfrac{3}{7}$

c) $\dfrac{3}{17} + \dfrac{1}{17} + \dfrac{4}{17}$

d) $\dfrac{7}{9} - \dfrac{2}{9}$

e) $\dfrac{11}{21} - \dfrac{9}{21}$

f) $\dfrac{2}{5} + \dfrac{4}{5} - \dfrac{3}{5}$

2. Add or subtract (change *both* denominators).

a) $\dfrac{3}{5} + \dfrac{1}{2}$

b) $\dfrac{4}{5} + \dfrac{1}{2}$

c) $\dfrac{1}{5} + \dfrac{2}{3}$

d) $\dfrac{1}{2} - \dfrac{1}{3}$

e) $\dfrac{2}{3} + \dfrac{3}{4}$

f) $\dfrac{4}{5} - \dfrac{1}{4}$

3. Add or subtract (change *one* denominator).

a) $\dfrac{1}{3} + \dfrac{1}{6}$

b) $\dfrac{1}{5} + \dfrac{1}{20}$

c) $\dfrac{1}{2} + \dfrac{1}{6}$

d) $\dfrac{2}{3} + \dfrac{1}{15}$

e) $\dfrac{2}{5} + \dfrac{1}{10}$

f) $\dfrac{3}{4} + \dfrac{1}{2}$

F-6 HW:
Fractions

1.   a) Cut the pie into 2 pieces.   b) Cut the pie into 4 pieces.
                 Shade 1/2   Shade 1/4

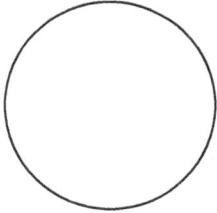

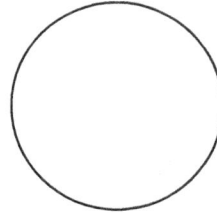

      c) Which piece of pie is bigger: 1/2 or 1/4? Why?

2. Add or subtract.

   a) $\dfrac{4}{7} - \dfrac{2}{7}$ b) $\dfrac{3}{11} + \dfrac{2}{11} + \dfrac{5}{11}$ c) $\dfrac{3}{4} - \dfrac{2}{4}$

3. Add or subtract (change *both* the denominators).

   a) $\dfrac{1}{3} + \dfrac{1}{5}$ b) $\dfrac{2}{3} + \dfrac{1}{2}$ c) $\dfrac{1}{2} - \dfrac{1}{5}$

4. Add or subtract (change *one* denominator).

   a) $\dfrac{1}{2} + \dfrac{1}{8}$ b) $\dfrac{1}{5} + \dfrac{1}{15}$ c) $\dfrac{1}{2} + \dfrac{1}{6}$

   d) $\dfrac{2}{5} + \dfrac{1}{20}$ e) $\dfrac{2}{5} - \dfrac{3}{10}$ f) $\dfrac{1}{3} - \dfrac{1}{12}$

5.   Advanced: Add or subtract (change *one* denominator or change *both* ** for each question you have to decide what to do**),

   a) $\dfrac{1}{2} + \dfrac{1}{10}$ b) $\dfrac{2}{3} + \dfrac{1}{2}$ c) $\dfrac{1}{4} + \dfrac{1}{12}$

F-8 HW:
Fractions

1. Add or subtract: change *one* denominator, change *both,* or don't change *either*.

   a) $\dfrac{1}{3} - \dfrac{1}{5}$
       b) $\dfrac{1}{2} + \dfrac{1}{6}$
       c) $\dfrac{1}{7} + \dfrac{3}{7}$

   d) $\dfrac{1}{5} + \dfrac{3}{20}$
       e) $\dfrac{1}{3} + \dfrac{1}{9}$
       f) $\dfrac{2}{3} - \dfrac{1}{2}$

   g) $\dfrac{1}{3} + \dfrac{1}{12}$
       h) $\dfrac{2}{5} + \dfrac{3}{25}$
       i) $\dfrac{1}{11} + \dfrac{5}{11}$

2. Reduce.

   a) $\dfrac{2}{10}$
       b) $\dfrac{3}{9}$
       c) $\dfrac{4}{8}$
       d) $\dfrac{5}{20}$

   e) $\dfrac{2}{6}$
       f) $\dfrac{5}{15}$
       g) $\dfrac{3}{12}$
       h) $\dfrac{4}{12}$

3. Advanced: Reduce.

   a) $\dfrac{4}{6}$
       b) $\dfrac{6}{8}$
       c) $\dfrac{10}{15}$
       d) $\dfrac{20}{25}$

   e) $\dfrac{6}{9}$
       f) $\dfrac{15}{30}$
       g) $\dfrac{12}{15}$
       h) $\dfrac{4}{10}$

4. Add.

   a) $\dfrac{1}{2} + \dfrac{1}{3} + \dfrac{1}{6}$
       b) $\dfrac{1}{3} + \dfrac{1}{5} + \dfrac{1}{15}$

   BONUS:

   c) $\dfrac{1}{2} + \dfrac{1}{3} - \dfrac{1}{6}$
       d) $\dfrac{1}{2} + \dfrac{1}{8} + \dfrac{1}{4}$

F-12 HW:
Mixed and Improper Fractions

1. Add or subtract: change *one* denominator, change *both,* or don't change *either.*

    a) $\dfrac{1}{2} + \dfrac{1}{3}$

    b) $\dfrac{3}{4} - \dfrac{1}{2}$

    c) $\dfrac{1}{11} + \dfrac{2}{11}$

    d) $\dfrac{2}{5} + \dfrac{1}{4}$

    e) $\dfrac{1}{3} - \dfrac{1}{9}$

    f) $\dfrac{1}{5} + \dfrac{1}{25}$

2. Add.

    a) $\dfrac{1}{2} + \dfrac{1}{6} + \dfrac{3}{6}$

    b) $\dfrac{1}{11} + \dfrac{1}{11} + \dfrac{2}{11} =$

3. Change to an <u>improper</u> fraction.

    a) $2\dfrac{1}{2} =$ b) $3\dfrac{1}{3} =$ c) $5\dfrac{2}{3} =$ d) $3\dfrac{2}{5} =$ e) $4\dfrac{1}{5} =$ f) $5\dfrac{1}{6} =$

4. Divide.

    a) $2\,\overline{|\,7\,}$ b) $2\,\overline{|\,9\,}$ c) $3\,\overline{|\,11\,}$ d) $5\,\overline{|\,27\,}$ e) $5\,\overline{|\,8\,}$ f) $3\,\overline{|\,5\,}$

5. Change to a <u>mixed</u> fraction.

    a) $\dfrac{7}{2} =$

    b) $\dfrac{11}{3} =$

    c) $\dfrac{17}{5} =$

    d) $\dfrac{21}{4} =$

PRACTICE TEST – Level C:

1. Name these fractions:

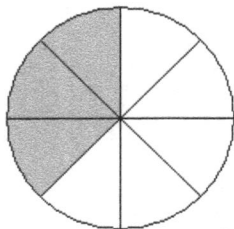

2. Add or subtract:

$$\frac{1}{7} + \frac{2}{7} \qquad\qquad \frac{3}{5} + \frac{1}{5} \qquad\qquad \frac{3}{11} + \frac{5}{11}$$

$$\frac{4}{5} + \frac{1}{2} \qquad\qquad \frac{1}{3} + \frac{1}{2} \qquad\qquad \frac{1}{2} + \frac{1}{10}$$

$$\frac{1}{3} - \frac{1}{9} \qquad\qquad \frac{1}{2} + \frac{1}{3} + \frac{1}{6}$$

3. Reduce: $\dfrac{5}{15} =$ $\dfrac{4}{6} =$

$$\frac{3}{9} = \qquad\qquad \frac{20}{25} =$$

PRACTICE TEST – Level C (continued):

4. Name these fractions as <u>mixed</u> fractions:

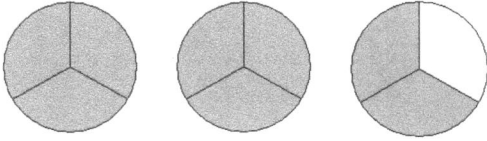

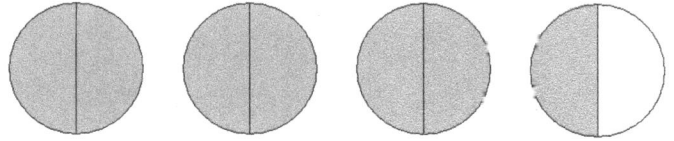

5. Name these fractions as <u>improper</u> fractions:

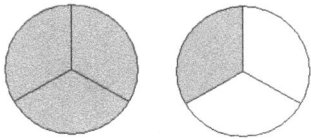

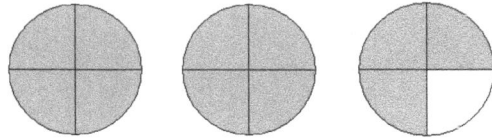

6. Draw these <u>mixed</u> fractions:

   $2\frac{1}{4}$ $3\frac{1}{2}$

7. Draw these <u>improper</u> fractions:

   $\frac{5}{2}$ $\frac{7}{4}$

FINAL TEST – Level C:

1. Name these fractions:

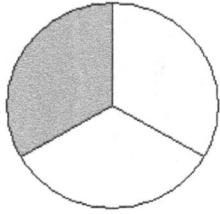

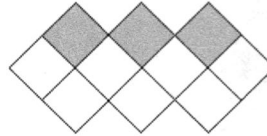

2. Add or subtract:

$$\frac{1}{5} \ + \ \frac{2}{5} \qquad\qquad \frac{3}{11} \ + \ \frac{1}{11} \qquad\qquad \frac{3}{17} \ + \ \frac{5}{17}$$

$$\frac{1}{3} \ + \ \frac{1}{2} \qquad\qquad \frac{1}{3} \ + \ \frac{1}{5} \qquad\qquad \frac{1}{2} \ + \ \frac{1}{6}$$

$$\frac{1}{3} \ - \ \frac{1}{9} \qquad\qquad \frac{1}{2} \ + \ \frac{1}{5} \ + \ \frac{1}{10}$$

3. Reduce: $\qquad \dfrac{3}{15} \ = \qquad\qquad \dfrac{4}{6} \ =$

$$\qquad\qquad\quad \frac{3}{9} \ = \qquad\qquad \frac{20}{25} \ =$$

FINAL TEST – Level C (continued):

4. Name these fractions as <u>mixed</u> fractions:

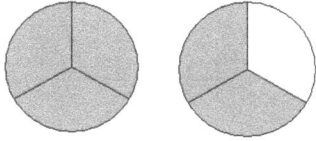

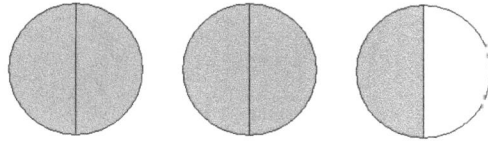

5. Name these fractions as <u>improper</u> fractions:

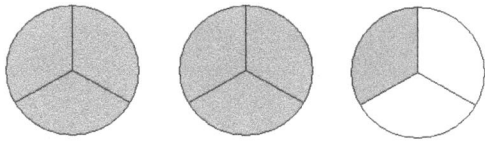

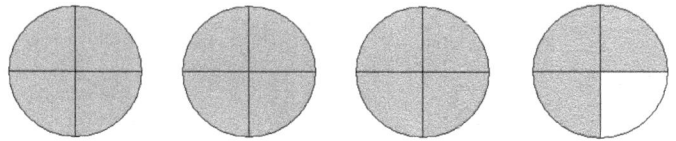

6. Draw these <u>mixed</u> fractions:

$3\frac{1}{4}$ $2\frac{1}{2}$

7. Draw these <u>improper</u> fractions:

$\frac{7}{2}$ $\frac{5}{4}$

PRACTICE TEST – Level D:

1. Name these fractions:

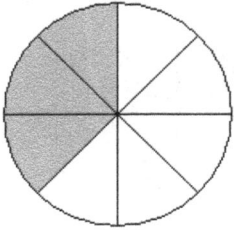

2. Add or subtract:

$$\frac{1}{7} + \frac{2}{7} \qquad\qquad \frac{3}{5} + \frac{1}{5} \qquad\qquad \frac{5}{11} - \frac{3}{11}$$

$$\frac{4}{5} + \frac{1}{2} \qquad\qquad \frac{1}{3} + \frac{1}{2} \qquad\qquad \frac{1}{2} + \frac{1}{10}$$

$$\frac{1}{3} - \frac{1}{9} \qquad\qquad \text{BONUS:} \quad \frac{1}{2} + \frac{1}{3} + \frac{1}{6}$$

3. Reduce:
$$\frac{5}{15} \qquad\qquad \frac{4}{6}$$

$$\frac{3}{9} \qquad\qquad \frac{20}{25}$$

PRACTICE TEST – Level D (continued):

4. Convert to an improper fraction: $3\frac{1}{3}$ $1\frac{3}{5}$

5. Convert to a mixed fraction: $\frac{7}{2}$ $\frac{8}{3}$

6. Add: $1\frac{1}{3}$ + $2\frac{1}{2}$ $2\frac{1}{2}$ + $\frac{2}{3}$

7. Circle the bigger fraction in each pair (make the denominators the same first):

$\frac{1}{2}$ $\frac{3}{10}$ $\frac{2}{3}$ $\frac{4}{5}$

8. Jane ate $\frac{3}{8}$ of a pizza and Tom ate $\frac{1}{4}$. What fraction of the pizza did they eat?

FINAL TEST – Level D:

1. Name these fractions:

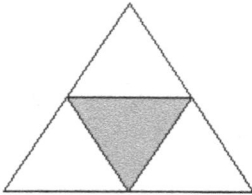

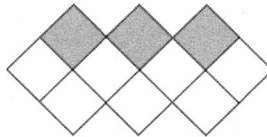

2. Add or subtract:

$$\frac{1}{8} + \frac{3}{8} \qquad\qquad \frac{3}{5} - \frac{1}{5} \qquad\qquad \frac{2}{12} + \frac{5}{12}$$

$$\frac{2}{5} + \frac{1}{2} \qquad\qquad \frac{2}{3} + \frac{1}{5} \qquad\qquad \frac{1}{3} + \frac{2}{12}$$

$$\frac{3}{5} - \frac{2}{20} \qquad\qquad \text{BONUS:} \quad \frac{1}{3} + \frac{1}{5} + \frac{1}{15}$$

3. Reduce:

$$\frac{5}{20} \qquad\qquad \frac{6}{9}$$

$$\frac{2}{8} \qquad\qquad \frac{15}{25}$$

FINAL TEST – Level D (continued):

4. Convert to an improper fraction: $4\frac{1}{2}$ $2\frac{2}{5}$

5. Convert to a mixed fraction: $\frac{7}{3}$ $\frac{9}{2}$

6. Add: $1\frac{1}{2}$ + $1\frac{2}{3}$ $1\frac{1}{3}$ + $\frac{1}{5}$

7. Circle the bigger fraction in each pair (make the denominators the same first):

   $\frac{1}{3}$ $\frac{4}{9}$ $\frac{1}{2}$ $\frac{3}{5}$

8. Jane ate $\frac{1}{3}$ of a pizza and Tom ate $\frac{3}{5}$. What fraction of the pizza did they eat?

TESTS *(Level C)*:
Marking Scheme

Question 1: 2 parts – 4 pts each   - 2 pts numerator correct   8
- 2 pts denominator correct

Question 2: 7 parts – 4 pts each   - 1 pt correct method   28
- 2 pts correct conversion to same denom.
- 1 pt correct add/sub answer

              BONUS – 8 pts   - 2 pt correct method   8
- 4 pts correct conversion to same denom.
- 2 pt correct add/sub answer

Question 3: 4 parts – 4 pts each   - 2 pts correct divisor   16
- 1 pt numerator correct (based on divisor chosen)
- 1 pt denominator correct (based on divisor chosen)

Question 4: 2 parts – 5 pts each   - 3 pts correct whole number   10
- 2 pt correct fraction

Question 5: 2 parts – 5 pts each   - 3 pts numerator correct   10
- 2 pts denominator correct

Question 6: 2 parts – 5 pts each   - 2 pts correct number of pies   10
- 2 pts correct # of subdivisions in each piece
- 1 pt correct fractional pie on end

Question 7: 2 parts – 5 pts each   - 2 pts correct number of pies   10
- 2 pts correct # of subdivisions in each piece
- 1 pt correct fractional pie on end

Total: 100 pts

TESTS *(Level D)*:
Marking Scheme

<u>Points</u>

Question 1: 2 parts – 4 pts each   - 2 pts numerator correct   8
- 2 pts denominator correct

Question 2: 7 parts – 4 pts each   - 1 pt correct method   28
- 2 pts correct conversion to same denom.
- 1 pt correct add/sub answer

          BONUS – 5 pts   - 1 pt correct method   5
- 3 pts correct conversion to same denom.
- 1 pt correct add/sub answer

Question 3: 4 parts – 4 pts each   - 2 pts correct divisor   16
- 1 pt numerator correct (based on divisor chosen)
- 1 pt denominator correct (based on divisor chosen)

Question 4: 2 parts – 4 pts each   - 2 pts correct numerator   8
    (1 pt correct x, 1 pt correct +)
- 2 pt correct denominator

Question 5: 2 parts – 4 pts each   - 2 pts whole number   8
- 1 pt numerator correct
- 1 pt denominator correct

Question 6: 2 parts – 6 pts each   - 2 pts correct conversion to improper   12
- 2 pts correct conversion to same denom.
- 2 pt correct add/sub answer

Question 7: 2 parts – 4 pts each   - 1 pt correct method   8
- 2 pts correct conversion to same denom.
- 1 pt correct < or > answer

Question 8: 1 part – 7 pts   - 2 pts correct equation   7
- 1 pt correct method
- 2 pt correct conversion to same denom.
- 2 pt correct add/sub answer

Total: 100 pts

Answer Key: Fractions Challenge – Level C

NOTE: Not all questions in on the worksheets are labelled with an a) or b), etc. For clarity in the answer key, we have adopted this labelling. It should be easy to tell which answer goes with a particular question – even if it is not marked with a letter on the worksheet.

Worksheet F-1

Teacher to check that hands are completed properly.

1. a) 6
   b) 2
   c) 8
   d) 6
   e) 2
   f) 10
   g) 4
   h) 8
2. a) 9
   b) 6
   c) 12
   d) 9
   e) 3
   f) 9
   g) 15
   h) 6
3. a) 15
   b) 10
   c) 20
   d) 15
   e) 5
   f) 15
   g) 25
   h) 10
4. a) 9
   b) 4
   c) 20
   d) 8
   e) 5

f) 15
g) 10
h) 15
i) 6
j) 6
k) 12
l) 4
m) 3
n) 15
o) 20
p) 25
q) 15
r) 2
s) 4
t) 5

BONUS:
u) 8
v) 21
w) 23
x) 296
y) 663
z) 0
aa) 1
bb) 12 035
cc) 46
dd) 127
ee) 0
ff) 0
gg) 1905
hh) 0
ii) 0
jj) 6

Worksheet F-2

1. a) $\frac{1}{2}$
   b) $\frac{1}{4}$
   c) $\frac{2}{3}$
   d) $\frac{1}{3}$
   e) $\frac{3}{8}$
   f) $\frac{3}{4}$

g) $\frac{1}{4}$
h) $\frac{5}{6}$
i) $\frac{5}{9}$
j) $\frac{7}{10}$
k) $\frac{1}{8}$
l) $\frac{3}{10}$

2. Teacher to check.

Worksheet F-3 A

1. a) $\frac{2}{3}$
   b) $\frac{5}{7}$
   c) $\frac{3}{11}$
   d) $\frac{4}{5}$
   e) $\frac{5}{11}$
   f) $\frac{7}{8}$
   g) $\frac{5}{17}$
   h) $\frac{5}{21}$
   i) $\frac{7}{9}$
2. a) $\frac{2}{5}$
   b) $\frac{1}{7}$
   c) $\frac{2}{11}$
   d) $\frac{3}{8}$
   e) $\frac{4}{17}$
   f) $\frac{4}{9}$
3. a) $\frac{3}{7}$
   b) $\frac{6}{7}$
   c) $\frac{8}{15}$

BONUS:
d) $\frac{4}{11}$

Worksheet F-3 B

1. a) $\frac{3}{4}$
   b) $\frac{6}{7}$
   c) $\frac{10}{11}$
   d) $\frac{11}{17}$
   e) $\frac{16}{19}$
   f) $\frac{25}{32}$
2. a) $\frac{6}{11}$
   b) $\frac{1}{10}$
   c) $\frac{7}{15}$
   d) $\frac{3}{19}$
   e) $\frac{13}{17}$
   f) $\frac{4}{9}$
3. a) $\frac{6}{7}$
   b) $\frac{16}{17}$
   c) $\frac{11}{12}$

BONUS:
d) $\frac{5}{11}$
e) $\frac{6}{11}$
f) $\frac{15}{35}$

Worksheet F-4 A

1. Teacher to check.
2. Teacher to check.
3. Teacher to check.
4. Teacher to check.
5. a) $\frac{3}{6} + \frac{2}{6}$
   b) $\frac{5}{10} + \frac{2}{10}$
   c) $\frac{5}{15} + \frac{3}{15}$
   d) $\frac{4}{6} + \frac{3}{6}$
   e) $\frac{10}{15} + \frac{3}{15}$

f) $\frac{6}{15} + \frac{5}{15}$

g) $\frac{6}{10} + \frac{5}{10}$

h) $\frac{8}{10} + \frac{5}{10}$

i) $\frac{10}{15} + \frac{6}{15}$

6. a) $\frac{5}{6}$

b) $\frac{7}{10}$

c) $\frac{8}{15}$

d) $\frac{7}{6}$

e) $\frac{13}{15}$

f) $\frac{11}{15}$

g) $\frac{11}{10}$

h) $\frac{13}{10}$

i) $\frac{16}{15}$

7. a) $\frac{3}{6} + \frac{2}{6} = \frac{5}{6}$

b) $\frac{5}{10} + \frac{2}{10} = \frac{7}{10}$

c) $\frac{5}{15} + \frac{3}{15} = \frac{8}{15}$

d) $\frac{4}{6} + \frac{3}{6} = \frac{7}{6}$

e) $\frac{10}{15} + \frac{3}{15} = \frac{13}{15}$

f) $\frac{6}{15} + \frac{5}{15} = \frac{11}{15}$

g) $\frac{6}{10} + \frac{5}{10} = \frac{11}{10}$

h) $\frac{8}{10} + \frac{5}{10} = \frac{13}{10}$

i) $\frac{10}{15} + \frac{6}{15} = \frac{16}{15}$

8. a) $\frac{5}{6}$

b) $\frac{8}{15}$

c) $\frac{7}{10}$

9. a) $\frac{11}{15}$

b) $\frac{11}{10}$

c) $\frac{7}{6}$

d) $\frac{13}{15}$

e) $\frac{13}{10}$

f) $\frac{16}{15}$

BONUS:

g) $\frac{1}{6}$

h) $\frac{1}{6}$

i) $\frac{1}{10}$

Worksheet F-4 B

1. a) $\frac{8}{15}$

b) $\frac{7}{12}$

c) $\frac{11}{30}$

2. a) $\frac{23}{20}$

b) $\frac{13}{15}$

c) $\frac{17}{30}$

d) $\frac{31}{20}$

e) $\frac{31}{30}$

f) $\frac{17}{12}$

BONUS:

g) $\frac{1}{12}$

h) $\frac{7}{20}$

i) $\frac{7}{30}$

Worksheet F-4 C

1. a) $\frac{10}{21}$

b) $\frac{13}{40}$

c) $\frac{13}{36}$

2. a) $\frac{17}{21}$

b) $\frac{28}{45}$

c) $\frac{37}{42}$

d) $\frac{29}{28}$

e) $\frac{19}{24}$

f) $\frac{37}{63}$

BONUS:

g) $\frac{17}{28}$

h) $\frac{19}{56}$

i) $\frac{26}{63}$

Worksheet F-5 A

1. a) Multiply by 5

b) Multiply by 2

c) Multiply by 4

d) Multiply by 2

e) Multiply by 4

f) Multiply by 3

g) Multiply by 5

h) Multiply by 3

i) Multiply by 4

2. a) $\frac{5}{10} + \frac{1}{10}$

b) $\frac{2}{10} + \frac{1}{10}$

c) $\frac{4}{8} + \frac{1}{8}$

d) $\frac{2}{6} + \frac{1}{6}$

e) $\frac{4}{20} + \frac{1}{20}$

f) $\frac{3}{6} + \frac{1}{6}$

g) $\frac{10}{25} + \frac{1}{25}$

h) $\frac{9}{15} + \frac{1}{15}$

i) $\frac{4}{8} + \frac{7}{8}$

3. a) $\frac{6}{10}$

b) $\frac{3}{10}$

c) $\frac{5}{8}$

d) $\frac{3}{6}$

e) $\frac{5}{20}$

f) $\frac{4}{6}$

4. a) $\frac{11}{15}$

b) $\frac{5}{10}$

c) $\frac{11}{15}$

d) $\frac{9}{12}$

e) $\frac{5}{8}$

f) $\frac{6}{12}$

g) $\frac{5}{4}$

h) $\frac{9}{25}$

i) $\frac{15}{15}$

BONUS:

j) $\frac{3}{20}$

k) $\frac{1}{8}$

l) $\frac{2}{10}$

Worksheet F-5 B

1. a) $\frac{4}{12}$

b) $\frac{4}{18}$

c) $\frac{5}{28}$

2. a) $\frac{5}{16}$

b) $\frac{10}{21}$

c) $\frac{6}{24}$

d) $\frac{5}{18}$

e) $\frac{32}{30}$

f) $\frac{10}{24}$

g) $\frac{14}{27}$

h) $\frac{9}{12}$

i) $\frac{29}{42}$

BONUS:

j) $\frac{13}{16}$

k) $\dfrac{2}{21}$

l) $\dfrac{37}{48}$

Worksheet F-6 A

1. a) Yes
   b) No
   c) No
   d) Yes
   e) Yes
   f) Yes
   g) No
   h) No
2. a) Yes
   b) No
   c) Yes
   d) No
   e) Yes
   f) No
   g) No
   h) No
3. a) Yes
   b) No
   c) Yes
   d) No
   e) Yes
   f) No
   g) No
   h) No
4. b) Circle 3
   c) Circle 2
   d) Circle 4
   e) Circle 2
   f) Circle 2
5. b) No
   c) Yes
   d) Yes; Circle 4
   e) No; Circle 2
   f) Yes; Circle 2
   g) Yes; Circle 2
   h) No; Circle 3
   i) No; Circle 5
6. a) 3
   b) 2
   c) 3

7. a) 3, 2
   b) 5, 2
   c) 5, 3
8. a) No; 5, 3
   b) Yes; 2
   c) Yes; 2
   d) No; 4, 3
   BONUS:
   e) Yes; 3
   f) Yes; 2
9. a) No; $\dfrac{9}{20}$
   b) No; $\dfrac{13}{15}$
   c) Yes; $\dfrac{9}{20}$
   BONUS:
   d) Yes; $\dfrac{19}{20}$
   e) Yes; $\dfrac{11}{15}$
   f) Yes; $\dfrac{5}{16}$

Worksheet F-6 B

1. a) $\dfrac{4}{9}$
   b) $\dfrac{13}{15}$
   c) $\dfrac{5}{20}$
   d) $\dfrac{5}{6}$
   e) $\dfrac{9}{20}$
   f) $\dfrac{4}{10}$
   g) $\dfrac{9}{16}$
   h) $\dfrac{8}{20}$
   i) $\dfrac{7}{12}$
2. a) $\dfrac{5}{12}$
   b) $\dfrac{17}{20}$
   c) Same; $\dfrac{2}{7}$
   d) $\dfrac{7}{6}$

e) Same; $\dfrac{10}{11}$

f) $\dfrac{19}{20}$

Worksheet F-6 C

1. a) $\dfrac{2}{12}$
   b) $\dfrac{4}{7}$
   c) $\dfrac{22}{15}$
   d) $\dfrac{2}{25}$
   e) $\dfrac{6}{12}$
   f) $\dfrac{6}{14}$
   g) $\dfrac{4}{18}$
   h) $\dfrac{15}{40}$
   i) $\dfrac{11}{24}$
   j) $\dfrac{11}{30}$
   k) $\dfrac{2}{21}$
   l) $\dfrac{11}{24}$
   m) $\dfrac{19}{42}$
   n) $\dfrac{13}{28}$
   o) $\dfrac{9}{16}$
   BONUS:
   p) $\dfrac{59}{56}$
   q) $\dfrac{13}{27}$
   r) $\dfrac{17}{32}$

Worksheet F-7 A

1. a) 3, 2, -
   b) 5, 3, -
   c) 4, 2, -
   d) 5, 4, -
   e) 4, 3, -
   f) 4, 2, -
2. a) $\dfrac{3}{6} + \dfrac{2}{6} + \dfrac{1}{6}$
   b) $\dfrac{5}{15} + \dfrac{3}{15} + \dfrac{1}{15}$

c) $\dfrac{4}{8} + \dfrac{2}{8} + \dfrac{3}{8}$

d) $\dfrac{5}{20} + \dfrac{4}{20} + \dfrac{1}{20}$

e) $\dfrac{8}{12} + \dfrac{3}{12} + \dfrac{1}{12}$

f) $\dfrac{4}{20} + \dfrac{6}{20} + \dfrac{2}{20}$

3. a) $\dfrac{8}{6}$
   b) $\dfrac{9}{15}$
   c) $\dfrac{9}{8}$
   d) $\dfrac{14}{20}$
   e) $\dfrac{12}{12}$
   f) $\dfrac{12}{20}$
   BONUS:
   g) $\dfrac{6}{6}$
   h) $\dfrac{12}{12}$
   i) $\dfrac{11}{8}$
   j) $\dfrac{10}{20}$

Worksheet F-8 A

1. a) 2
   b) 3
   c) 4
   d) 5
   e) 1
   f) 4
   g) 2
   h) 1
   i) 3
   j) 5
   k) 2
   l) 3
   m) 5
   n) 4
   o) 1
   p) 2
   q) 3
   r) 4
   s) 5
   t) 1

2. Teacher to check.
3. Teacher to check.
4. a) $\frac{1}{2}$
   b) $\frac{1}{3}$
   c) $\frac{1}{5}$
   d) $\frac{1}{4}$
   e) $\frac{1}{5}$
   f) $\frac{1}{3}$
   g) $\frac{1}{2}$
   h) $\frac{1}{4}$
5. a) $\frac{1}{2}$
   b) $\frac{1}{3}$
   c) $\frac{1}{5}$
   d) $\frac{1}{4}$
   e) $\frac{1}{5}$
   f) $\frac{1}{3}$
   g) $\frac{1}{2}$
   h) $\frac{1}{4}$
   i) $\frac{1}{2}$
   j) $\frac{1}{5}$
   k) $\frac{1}{4}$
   l) $\frac{1}{3}$
   m) $\frac{1}{2}$
   n) $\frac{1}{3}$
   o) $\frac{1}{5}$
   p) $\frac{1}{4}$
6. a) $\frac{2}{3}$
   b) $\frac{4}{5}$
   c) $\frac{3}{4}$

   d) $\frac{2}{5}$
   e) $\frac{2}{3}$
   f) $\frac{4}{5}$
   g) $\frac{3}{4}$
   h) $\frac{2}{5}$
   i) $\frac{2}{3}$
   j) $\frac{3}{4}$
   k) $\frac{2}{5}$
   l) $\frac{3}{5}$
   BONUS:
   m) $\frac{5}{6}$
   n) $\frac{4}{5}$
   o) $\frac{5}{6}$
   p) $\frac{2}{3}$

Worksheet F-8 B
1. a) $\frac{1}{2}$
   b) $\frac{1}{3}$
   c) $\frac{1}{5}$
   d) $\frac{1}{4}$
   e) $\frac{\ }{3}$
   f) $\frac{1}{2}$
   g) $\frac{1}{4}$
   h) $\frac{1}{6}$
   i) $\frac{1}{2}$
   j) $\frac{1}{3}$
   k) $\frac{1}{5}$
   l) $\frac{1}{6}$
   m) $\frac{1}{3}$
   n) $\frac{1}{1} = 1$

   o) $\frac{1}{4}$
   p) $\frac{1}{6}$
2. a) $\frac{2}{3}$
   b) $\frac{3}{4}$
   c) $\frac{2}{3}$
   d) $\frac{2}{3}$
   e) $\frac{3}{4}$
   f) $\frac{4}{5}$
   g) $\frac{3}{4}$
   h) $\frac{5}{6}$
   BONUS:
   i) $\frac{10}{20} = \frac{1}{2}$
   j) $\frac{10}{12} = \frac{5}{6}$

Worksheet F-10 A
1. a) $\frac{3}{4}$
   b) $\frac{1}{8}$
   c) $\frac{1}{3}$
   d) $\frac{1}{2}$
   e) $\frac{2}{3}$
   f) $\frac{4}{5}$
   g) $\frac{1}{4}$
   h) $\frac{3}{8}$
2. a) 2
   b) 1
   c) 1
   d) 2
   e) 3
   f) 1
   g) 4
   h) 1

3. a) $2\frac{1}{2}$
   b) $1\frac{1}{4}$
   c) $1\frac{2}{3}$
   d) $2\frac{3}{8}$
   e) $3\frac{3}{4}$
   f) $4\frac{1}{2}$
   g) $3\frac{1}{3}$
   h) $2\frac{1}{8}$
   i) $4\frac{4}{5}$
4. a) $\frac{5}{2}$
   b) $\frac{5}{4}$
   c) $\frac{5}{3}$
   d) $\frac{19}{8}$
   e) $\frac{15}{4}$
   f) $\frac{9}{2}$
   g) $\frac{10}{3}$
   h) $\frac{15}{8}$
   i) $\frac{13}{6}$

Worksheet F-10 B
1. a) $3\frac{1}{2}$, $\frac{7}{2}$
   b) $2\frac{3}{4}$, $\frac{11}{4}$
   c) $2\frac{1}{3}$, $\frac{7}{3}$
   d) $3\frac{1}{8}$, $\frac{25}{8}$
   e) $3\frac{1}{4}$, $\frac{13}{4}$
   f) $4\frac{1}{2}$, $\frac{9}{2}$
   g) $1\frac{1}{2}$, $\frac{3}{2}$
   h) $3\frac{2}{3}$, $\frac{11}{3}$
   i) $1\frac{7}{8}$, $\frac{15}{8}$

j) $1\dfrac{1}{8}, \dfrac{9}{8}$

k) $1\dfrac{1}{4}, \dfrac{5}{4}$

l) $1\dfrac{4}{6}, \dfrac{10}{6}$

m) $2\dfrac{4}{5}, \dfrac{14}{5}$

2. a) $2\dfrac{5}{6}, \dfrac{17}{6}$

b) $3\dfrac{1}{8}, \dfrac{25}{8}$

c) $2\dfrac{1}{3}, \dfrac{7}{3}$

d) $2\dfrac{3}{8}, \dfrac{19}{8}$

e) $3\dfrac{3}{10}, \dfrac{33}{10}$

f) $3\dfrac{7}{10}, \dfrac{37}{10}$

g) $1\dfrac{5}{9}, \dfrac{14}{9}$

h) $3\dfrac{1}{3}, \dfrac{10}{3}$

i) $2\dfrac{1}{2}, \dfrac{5}{2}$

j) $\dfrac{16}{15} \quad 1\dfrac{1}{3}, \dfrac{4}{3}$

k) $2\dfrac{1}{4}, \dfrac{9}{4}$

Worksheet F-10 C

1. a)

b)

c)

d)

e)

f)

g)

h)

2. a)

b)

c)

d)

e)

f)

3. a)

b)

c)

d)

e)

f)

g)

h)

4. a)

b)

c)

d)

e)

f)

Answer Key: Fractions Challenge – Level D

NOTE: Not all questions on the worksheets are labelled with an a) or b), etc.

For clarity in the answer key, we have adopted this labelling. It should be easy to tell which answer goes with a particular question – even if it is not marked with a letter on the worksheet.

Worksheet F-1

Teacher to check that hands are completed properly.

1. a) 6
   b) 2
   c) 8
   d) 6
   e) 2
   f) 10
   g) 4
   h) 8
2. a) 9
   b) 6
   c) 12
   d) 9
   e) 3
   f) 9
   g) 15
   h) 6
3. a) 15
   b) 10
   c) 20
   d) 15
   e) 5
   f) 15
   g) 25
   h) 10
4. a) 9
   b) 4
   c) 20
   d) 8

e) 5
f) 15
g) 10
h) 15
i) 6
j) 6
k) 12
l) 4
m) 3
n) 15
o) 20
p) 25
q) 15
r) 2
s) 4
t) 5

BONUS:
u) 8
v) 21
w) 23
x) 296
y) 663
z) 0
aa) 1
bb) 12 035
cc) 46
dd) 127
ee) 0
ff) 0
gg) 1905
hh) 0
ii) 0
jj) 6

Worksheet F-2

1. a) $\frac{1}{2}$
   b) $\frac{1}{4}$
   c) $\frac{2}{3}$
   d) $\frac{1}{3}$
   e) $\frac{3}{8}$
   f) $\frac{3}{4}$

g) $\frac{1}{4}$
h) $\frac{5}{6}$
i) $\frac{5}{9}$
j) $\frac{7}{10}$
k) $\frac{1}{8}$
l) $\frac{3}{10}$

2. Teacher to check.

Worksheet F-3 A

1. a) $\frac{2}{3}$
   b) $\frac{5}{7}$
   c) $\frac{3}{11}$
   d) $\frac{4}{5}$
   e) $\frac{5}{11}$
   f) $\frac{7}{8}$
   g) $\frac{5}{17}$
   h) $\frac{5}{21}$
   i) $\frac{7}{9}$
2. a) $\frac{2}{5}$
   b) $\frac{1}{7}$
   c) $\frac{2}{11}$
   d) $\frac{3}{8}$
   e) $\frac{4}{17}$
   f) $\frac{4}{9}$
3. a) $\frac{3}{7}$
   b) $\frac{6}{7}$
   c) $\frac{8}{15}$

BONUS:
d) $\frac{4}{11}$

Worksheet F-3 B

1. a) $\frac{3}{4}$
   b) $\frac{6}{7}$
   c) $\frac{10}{11}$
   d) $\frac{11}{17}$
   e) $\frac{16}{19}$
   f) $\frac{25}{32}$
2. a) $\frac{6}{11}$
   b) $\frac{1}{10}$
   c) $\frac{7}{15}$
   d) $\frac{3}{19}$
   e) $\frac{13}{17}$
   f) $\frac{4}{9}$
3. a) $\frac{6}{7}$
   b) $\frac{16}{17}$
   c) $\frac{11}{12}$

BONUS
   d) $\frac{5}{11}$
   e) $\frac{6}{11}$
   f) $\frac{15}{35}$

Worksheet F-4 A

1. Teacher to check.
2. Teacher to check.
3. Teacher to check.
4. Teacher to check.
5. a) $\frac{5}{6}$
   b) $\frac{7}{10}$
   c) $\frac{8}{15}$
   d) $\frac{7}{6}$

e) $\frac{13}{15}$

f) $\frac{11}{15}$

6. a) $\frac{5}{6}$

b) $\frac{7}{10}$

c) $\frac{8}{15}$

d) $\frac{7}{6}$

e) $\frac{13}{15}$

f) $\frac{11}{10}$

7. a) $\frac{5}{6}$

b) $\frac{8}{15}$

c) $\frac{7}{10}$

8. a) $\frac{11}{15}$

b) $\frac{11}{10}$

c) $\frac{7}{6}$

d) $\frac{13}{15}$

e) $\frac{13}{10}$

f) $\frac{16}{15}$

BONUS:

g) $\frac{1}{6}$

h) $\frac{1}{6}$

i) $\frac{1}{10}$

Worksheet F-4 B

1. a) $\frac{8}{15}$

b) $\frac{7}{12}$

c) $\frac{11}{30}$

2. a) $\frac{23}{20}$

b) $\frac{13}{15}$

c) $\frac{17}{30}$

d) $\frac{31}{20}$

e) $\frac{31}{30}$

f) $\frac{17}{12}$

BONUS:

g) $\frac{1}{12}$

h) $\frac{7}{20}$

i) $\frac{7}{30}$

Worksheet F-4 C

1. a) $\frac{10}{21}$

b) $\frac{13}{40}$

c) $\frac{13}{36}$

2. a) $\frac{17}{21}$

b) $\frac{28}{45}$

c) $\frac{37}{42}$

d) $\frac{29}{28}$

e) $\frac{19}{24}$

f) $\frac{37}{63}$

BONUS:

g) $\frac{17}{28}$

h) $\frac{19}{56}$

i) $\frac{26}{63}$

Worksheet F-5 A

1. a) Multiply by 5

b) Multiply by 2

c) Multiply by 4

d) Multiply by 2

e) Multiply by 4

f) Multiply by 3

g) Multiply by 5

h) Multiply by 3

i) Multiply by 4

2. a) $\frac{5}{10} + \frac{1}{10}$

b) $\frac{2}{10} + \frac{1}{10}$

c) $\frac{4}{8} + \frac{1}{8}$

d) $\frac{2}{6} + \frac{1}{6}$

e) $\frac{4}{20} + \frac{1}{20}$

f) $\frac{3}{6} + \frac{1}{6}$

g) $\frac{10}{25} + \frac{1}{25}$

h) $\frac{9}{15} + \frac{1}{15}$

i) $\frac{4}{8} + \frac{7}{8}$

3. a) $\frac{6}{10}$

b) $\frac{3}{10}$

c) $\frac{5}{8}$

d) $\frac{3}{6}$

e) $\frac{5}{20}$

f) $\frac{4}{6}$

4. a) $\frac{11}{15}$

b) $\frac{5}{10}$

c) $\frac{11}{15}$

d) $\frac{9}{12}$

e) $\frac{5}{8}$

f) $\frac{6}{12}$

g) $\frac{5}{4}$

h) $\frac{9}{25}$

i) $\frac{15}{15}$

BONUS:

j) $\frac{3}{20}$

k) $\frac{1}{8}$

l) $\frac{2}{10}$

Worksheet F-5 B

1. a) $\frac{4}{12}$

b) $\frac{4}{18}$

c) $\frac{5}{28}$

2. a) $\frac{5}{16}$

b) $\frac{10}{21}$

c) $\frac{6}{24}$

d) $\frac{5}{18}$

e) $\frac{32}{30}$

f) $\frac{10}{24}$

g) $\frac{14}{27}$

h) $\frac{9}{12}$

i) $\frac{29}{42}$

BONUS:

j) $\frac{13}{16}$

k) $\frac{2}{21}$

l) $\frac{37}{48}$

Worksheet F-6 A

1. a) Yes

b) No

c) No

d) Yes

e) Yes

f) Yes

g) No

h) No

2. a) Yes

b) No

c) Yes

d) No

e) Yes

f) No

g) No

h) No

3. a) Yes
    b) No
    c) Yes
    d) No
    e) Yes
    f) No
    g) No
    h) No
4. b) Circle 3
    c) Circle 2
    d) Circle 4
    e) Circle 2
    f) Circle 2
5. b) No
    c) Yes
    d) Yes; Circle 4
    e) No; Circle 2
    f) Yes; Circle 2
    g) Yes; Circle 2
    h) No; Circle 3
    i) No; Circle 5
6. a) 3
    b) 2
    c) 3
7. a) 3, 2
    b) 5, 2
    c) 5, 3
8. a) No; 5, 3
    b) Yes; 2
    c) Yes; 2
    d) No; 4, 3
    BONUS:
    e) Yes; 3
    f) Yes; 2
9. a) No; $\frac{9}{20}$
    b) No; $\frac{13}{15}$
    c) Yes; $\frac{9}{20}$
    BONUS:
    d) Yes; $\frac{19}{20}$

    e) Yes; $\frac{11}{15}$
    f) Yes; $\frac{5}{16}$

Worksheet F-6 B
1. a) $\frac{4}{9}$
    b) $\frac{13}{15}$
    c) $\frac{5}{20}$
    d) $\frac{5}{6}$
    e) $\frac{9}{20}$
    f) $\frac{4}{10}$
    g) $\frac{9}{16}$
    h) $\frac{8}{20}$
    i) $\frac{7}{12}$
2. a) $\frac{5}{12}$
    b) $\frac{17}{20}$
    c) Same; $\frac{2}{7}$
    d) $\frac{7}{6}$
    e) Same; $\frac{10}{11}$
    f) $\frac{19}{20}$

Worksheet F-6 C
1. a) $\frac{2}{12}$
    b) $\frac{4}{7}$
    c) $\frac{22}{15}$
    d) $\frac{2}{25}$
    e) $\frac{6}{12}$
    f) $\frac{6}{14}$
    g) $\frac{4}{18}$
    h) $\frac{15}{40}$
    i) $\frac{11}{24}$
    j) $\frac{11}{30}$

    k) $\frac{2}{21}$
    l) $\frac{11}{24}$
    m) $\frac{19}{42}$
    n) $\frac{13}{28}$
    o) $\frac{9}{16}$
    BONUS:
    p) $\frac{59}{56}$
    q) $\frac{13}{27}$
    r) $\frac{17}{32}$

Worksheet F-7 A
1. a) 3, 2, -
    b) 5, 3, -
    c) 4, 2, -
    d) 5, 4, -
    e) 4, 3, -
    f) 4, 2, -
2. a) $\frac{3}{6} + \frac{2}{6} + \frac{1}{6}$
    b) $\frac{5}{15} + \frac{3}{15} + \frac{1}{15}$
    c) $\frac{4}{8} + \frac{2}{8} + \frac{3}{8}$
    d) $\frac{5}{20} + \frac{4}{20} + \frac{1}{20}$
    e) $\frac{8}{12} + \frac{3}{12} + \frac{1}{12}$
    f) $\frac{4}{20} + \frac{6}{20} + \frac{2}{20}$
3. a) $\frac{8}{6}$
    b) $\frac{9}{15}$
    c) $\frac{9}{8}$
    d) $\frac{14}{20}$
    e) $\frac{12}{12}$
    f) $\frac{12}{20}$
    BONUS:
    g) $\frac{6}{6}$
    h) $\frac{12}{12}$

    i) $\frac{11}{8}$
    j) $\frac{10}{20}$

Worksheet F-8 A
1. a) 2
    b) 3
    c) 4
    d) 5
    e) 1
    f) 4
    g) 2
    h) 1
    i) 3
    j) 5
    k) 2
    l) 3
    m) 5
    n) 4
    o) 1
    p) 2
    q) 3
    r) 4
    s) 5
    t) 1
2. Teacher to check.
3. Teacher to check.
4. a) $\frac{1}{2}$
    b) $\frac{1}{3}$
    c) $\frac{1}{5}$
    d) $\frac{1}{2}$
    e) $\frac{1}{5}$
    f) $\frac{1}{3}$
    g) $\frac{1}{2}$
    h) $\frac{1}{4}$
5. a) $\frac{1}{2}$
    b) $\frac{1}{3}$
    c) $\frac{1}{5}$

d) $\frac{1}{4}$

e) $\frac{1}{5}$

f) $\frac{1}{3}$

g) $\frac{1}{2}$

h) $\frac{1}{4}$

i) $\frac{1}{2}$

j) $\frac{1}{5}$

k) $\frac{1}{4}$

l) $\frac{1}{3}$

m) $\frac{1}{2}$

n) $\frac{1}{3}$

o) $\frac{1}{5}$

p) $\frac{1}{4}$

6. a) $\frac{2}{3}$

b) $\frac{4}{5}$

c) $\frac{3}{4}$

d) $\frac{2}{5}$

e) $\frac{2}{3}$

f) $\frac{4}{5}$

g) $\frac{3}{4}$

h) $\frac{2}{5}$

i) $\frac{2}{3}$

j) $\frac{3}{4}$

k) $\frac{2}{5}$

l) $\frac{3}{5}$

BONUS:

m) $\frac{5}{6}$

n) $\frac{4}{5}$

o) $\frac{5}{6}$

p) $\frac{2}{3}$

Worksheet F-8 B

1. a) $\frac{1}{2}$

b) $\frac{1}{3}$

c) $\frac{1}{5}$

d) $\frac{1}{4}$

e) $\frac{1}{3}$

f) $\frac{1}{2}$

g) $\frac{1}{4}$

h) $\frac{1}{6}$

i) $\frac{1}{2}$

j) $\frac{1}{3}$

k) $\frac{1}{5}$

l) $\frac{1}{6}$

m) $\frac{1}{3}$

n) $\frac{1}{1} = 1$

o) $\frac{1}{4}$

p) $\frac{1}{6}$

2. a) $\frac{2}{3}$

b) $\frac{3}{4}$

c) $\frac{2}{3}$

d) $\frac{2}{3}$

e) $\frac{3}{4}$

f) $\frac{4}{5}$

g) $\frac{3}{4}$

h) $\frac{5}{6}$

BONUS:

i) $\frac{10}{20} = \frac{1}{2}$

j) $\frac{10}{12} = \frac{5}{6}$

Worksheet F-10 A

1. a) $\frac{3}{4}$

b) $\frac{1}{8}$

c) $\frac{1}{3}$

d) $\frac{1}{2}$

e) $\frac{2}{3}$

f) $\frac{4}{5}$

g) $\frac{1}{4}$

h) $\frac{3}{8}$

2. a) 2

b) 1

c) 1

d) 2

e) 3

f) 1

g) 4

h) 1

3. a) $2\frac{1}{2}$

b) $1\frac{1}{4}$

c) $1\frac{2}{3}$

d) $2\frac{3}{8}$

e) $3\frac{3}{4}$

f) $4\frac{1}{2}$

g) $3\frac{1}{3}$

h) $2\frac{1}{8}$

i) $4\frac{4}{5}$

4. a) $\frac{5}{2}$

b) $\frac{5}{4}$

c) $\frac{5}{3}$

d) $\frac{19}{8}$

e) $\frac{15}{4}$

f) $\frac{9}{2}$

g) $\frac{10}{3}$

h) $\frac{15}{8}$

i) $\frac{16}{6}$

Worksheet F-10 B

1. a) $3\frac{1}{2}$, $\frac{7}{2}$

b) $2\frac{3}{4}$, $\frac{11}{4}$

c) $2\frac{1}{3}$, $\frac{7}{3}$

d) $3\frac{1}{8}$, $\frac{25}{8}$

e) $3\frac{1}{4}$, $\frac{13}{4}$

f) $4\frac{1}{2}$, $\frac{9}{2}$

g) $1\frac{1}{2}$, $\frac{3}{2}$

h) $3\frac{2}{3}$, $\frac{11}{3}$

i) $1\frac{7}{8}$, $\frac{15}{8}$

j) $1\frac{1}{8}$, $\frac{9}{8}$

k) $1\frac{1}{4}$, $\frac{5}{4}$

l) $1\frac{4}{6}$, $\frac{10}{6}$

m) $2\frac{4}{5}$, $\frac{14}{5}$

2. a) $2\frac{5}{6}$, $\frac{17}{6}$

b) $3\frac{1}{8}$, $\frac{25}{8}$

c) $2\frac{1}{3}$, $\frac{7}{3}$

d) $2\frac{3}{8}$, $\frac{19}{8}$

e) $3\frac{3}{10}$, $\frac{33}{10}$

f) $3\frac{7}{10}$, $\frac{37}{10}$

g) $1\frac{5}{9}$, $\frac{14}{9}$

h) $3\frac{1}{3}$, $\frac{10}{3}$

i) $2\frac{1}{2}$, $\frac{5}{2}$

j) $1\frac{1}{3}$, $\frac{4}{3}$

k) $2\frac{1}{4}$, $\frac{9}{4}$

Worksheet F-10 C

1. a)
b)
c)
d)
e)
f)
g)
h)

2. a)
b)
c)
d)
e)
f)

3. a)
b)
c)
d)
e)
f)
g)
h)

4. a)
b)
c)

---

d)
e)
f)

Worksheet F-11 A

1. a) $\frac{5}{2}$

b) $\frac{3}{2}$

c) $\frac{10}{3}$

d) $\frac{11}{2}$

e) $\frac{11}{3}$

f) $\frac{7}{2}$

g) $\frac{13}{3}$

h) $\frac{17}{3}$

i) $\frac{16}{5}$

j) $\frac{17}{5}$

k) $\frac{26}{5}$

l) $\frac{14}{5}$

m) $\frac{9}{4}$

n) $\frac{5}{3}$

o) $\frac{7}{3}$

p) $\frac{16}{5}$

q) $\frac{13}{5}$

r) $\frac{7}{6}$

s) $\frac{7}{2}$

t) $\frac{19}{4}$

u) $\frac{11}{2}$

v) $\frac{10}{3}$

w) $\frac{17}{3}$

x) $\frac{11}{3}$

BONUS:

y) $\frac{11}{3}$

z) $\frac{22}{5}$

aa) $\frac{19}{3}$

bb) $\frac{13}{2}$

cc) $\frac{53}{5}$

dd) $\frac{19}{3}$

ee) $\frac{15}{2}$

ff) $\frac{32}{5}$

Worksheet F-11 B

1. a) $\frac{13}{4}$

b) $\frac{13}{6}$

c) $\frac{23}{7}$

d) $\frac{31}{6}$

e) $\frac{35}{8}$

f) $\frac{45}{7}$

g) $\frac{19}{2}$

h) $\frac{35}{4}$

i) $\frac{37}{7}$

j) $\frac{28}{9}$

k) $\frac{43}{9}$

l) $\frac{29}{8}$

m) $\frac{29}{4}$

n) $\frac{31}{6}$

o) $\frac{44}{7}$

p) $\frac{49}{6}$

q) $\frac{41}{4}$

r) $\frac{19}{6}$

s) $\frac{30}{7}$

---

t) $\frac{13}{6}$

BONUS:

u) $\frac{43}{8}$

v) $\frac{52}{7}$

w) $\frac{73}{8}$

x) $\frac{101}{12}$

y) $\frac{58}{7}$

z) $\frac{55}{6}$

aa) $\frac{52}{9}$

bb) $\frac{101}{8}$

Worksheet F-12 A

1. a) 2 R1
b) 3 R1
c) 4 R1
d) 5 R1
e) 1 R2
f) 2 R1
g) 3 R2
h) 4 R1
i) 5 R1
j) 9
k) 4 R1
l) 4 R2
m) 2 R1
n) 5 R2
o) 1 R1
p) 2 R1
q) 4 R1
r) 5 R1
s) 2 R3
t) 5 R2

2. a) $2\frac{1}{2}$

b) $4\frac{1}{2}$

c) $2\frac{1}{3}$

d) $3\frac{2}{3}$

e) $2\frac{2}{5}$

f) $3\frac{2}{5}$

g) $2\frac{2}{3}$

h) $4\frac{2}{5}$

i) $4\frac{1}{3}$

j) $5\frac{1}{5}$

k) $1\frac{2}{3}$

l) $4\frac{1}{5}$

m) $5\frac{1}{3}$

n) $5\frac{1}{2}$

o) $3\frac{1}{5}$

p) $2\frac{3}{5}$

BONUS:

q) $6\frac{1}{2}$

r) $6\frac{1}{5}$

s) $2\frac{1}{4}$

t) $4\frac{1}{3}$

3. a) 7 R1

b) 10 R1

c) 7 R1

d) 5 R2

e) 3 R3

f) 5 R2

g) 6 R1

h) 7 R2

4. a) $5\frac{2}{5}$

b) $7\frac{1}{4}$

c) $4\frac{1}{4}$

d) $9\frac{3}{5}$

e) $6\frac{2}{5}$

f) $5\frac{4}{5}$

BONUS:

g) $3\frac{1}{6}$

h) $3\frac{1}{9}$

i) $2\frac{1}{7}$

j) $2\frac{1}{8}$

Worksheet F-13 A

1. a) $\frac{17}{6} = 2\frac{5}{6}$

b) $\frac{23}{6} = 3\frac{5}{6}$

c) $\frac{27}{10} = 2\frac{7}{10}$

d) $\frac{13}{10} = 1\frac{3}{10}$

e) $\frac{17}{6} = 2\frac{5}{6}$

f) $\frac{27}{10} = 2\frac{7}{10}$

2. a) $\frac{2}{6} = \frac{1}{3}$

b) $\frac{21}{6} = 3\frac{3}{6} = 3\frac{1}{2}$

c) $\frac{25}{8} = 3\frac{1}{8}$

BONUS:

d) $\frac{22}{9} = 2\frac{4}{9}$

e) $\frac{21}{10} = 2\frac{1}{10}$

f) $\frac{16}{6} = 2\frac{4}{6} = 2\frac{2}{3}$

Worksheet F-13 B

1. a) $\frac{22}{6} = 3\frac{4}{6} = 3\frac{2}{3}$

b) $\frac{76}{9} = 8\frac{4}{9}$

c) $\frac{43}{6} = 7\frac{1}{6}$

d) $\frac{146}{15} = 9\frac{11}{15}$

e) $\frac{134}{20} = 6\frac{14}{20} = 6\frac{7}{10}$

f) $\frac{278}{35} = 7\frac{33}{35}$

g) $\frac{83}{8} = 10\frac{3}{8}$

h) $\frac{193}{30} = 6\frac{13}{30}$

i) $\frac{82}{21} = 3\frac{19}{21}$

BONUS:

j) $\frac{57}{6} = 9\frac{3}{6} = 9\frac{1}{2}$

k) $\frac{57}{16} = 3\frac{9}{16} = 3\frac{3}{4}$

l) $\frac{114}{15} = 7\frac{9}{15} = 7\frac{3}{5}$

Worksheet F-14 A

1. a) $\frac{3}{5}$

b) $\frac{5}{11}$

c) $\frac{3}{7}$

2. a) $\frac{2}{3}$

b) $\frac{4}{5}$

c) $\frac{3}{4}$

d) $\frac{1}{2}$

e) $\frac{3}{4}$

f) $\frac{1}{2}$

3. a) $\frac{7}{10}$

b) $\frac{5}{6}$

c) $\frac{4}{15}$

d) $\frac{2}{3}$

e) $\frac{3}{4}$

f) $\frac{2}{3}$

BONUS:

g) $\frac{3}{5}$

h) $\frac{4}{5}$

i) $\frac{2}{3}$

Worksheet F-15 A

1. a) They ate $\frac{5}{6}$ of a pie altogether.

b) They ate $\frac{8}{15}$ of a pie.

c) They ate $\frac{9}{10}$ of a pie.

d) They ate $\frac{5}{8}$ of a pizza.

Worksheet F-15 B

1. a) They ate $\frac{9}{20}$ of a pizza.

b) They ate $\frac{5}{9}$ of a pie.

c) They ate $\frac{5}{6}$ of a pie.

d) They ate $\frac{11}{16}$ of a pie.

BONUS:

e) They ate $\frac{6}{6}$ of a pizza altogether – this is equal to a whole pizza.

f) They ate $\frac{7}{8}$ of a pizza altogether.

Review (Sections F13-F15)

1. a) $\frac{26}{10} = 2\frac{6}{10} = 2\frac{3}{5}$

b) $\frac{31}{6} = 5\frac{1}{6}$

c) $\frac{7}{6} = 1\frac{1}{6}$

2. a) $\frac{3}{7}$

b) $\frac{3}{4}$

c) $\frac{1}{5}$

3. a) <

b) >

c) >

d) >

4. a) They ate $\frac{7}{6}$ of a pie which is greater than one pie.

b) They ate $\frac{8}{6} = \frac{4}{3}$ of a pizza, which is greater than one pizza.

Answer Key:

Sample Homework Pages

F-3 HW

1. a) $\frac{1}{4}$

   b) $\frac{2}{4}$

   c) $\frac{3}{4}$

2. a) $\frac{2}{3}$

   b) $\frac{5}{7}$

   c) $\frac{3}{11}$

   d) $\frac{11}{20}$

   e) $\frac{5}{6}$

   f) $\frac{8}{15}$

3. a) $\frac{3}{4}$

   b) $\frac{1}{8}$

   c) $\frac{5}{7}$

   BONUS:

   d) $\frac{4}{11}$

F-4 HW

1. a) $\frac{2}{4}$

   b) $\frac{3}{8}$

   c) $\frac{3}{6}$

2. a) $\frac{2}{3}$

   b) $\frac{5}{7}$

   c) $\frac{8}{15}$

   d) $\frac{2}{7}$

   e) $\frac{7}{11}$

   f) $\frac{5}{9}$

3. a) $\frac{5}{6}$

---

b) $\frac{8}{15}$

c) $\frac{7}{10}$

d) $\frac{11}{10}$

e) $\frac{13}{10}$

f) $\frac{13}{15}$

g) $\frac{1}{6}$

h) $\frac{1}{6}$

i) $\frac{1}{10}$

F-5 HW

1. a) $\frac{4}{5}$

   b) $\frac{5}{7}$

   c) $\frac{8}{17}$

   d) $\frac{5}{9}$

   e) $\frac{2}{21}$

   f) $\frac{3}{5}$

2. a) $\frac{11}{10}$

   b) $\frac{13}{10}$

   c) $\frac{13}{15}$

   d) $\frac{1}{6}$

   e) $\frac{17}{12}$

   f) $\frac{11}{20}$

3. a) $\frac{3}{6}$

   b) $\frac{5}{20}$

   c) $\frac{4}{6}$

   d) $\frac{11}{15}$

   e) $\frac{5}{10}$

   f) $\frac{5}{4}$

F-6 HW

1. a) Teacher to check.

   b) Teacher to check.

   c) Since both pies are the same size, the $\frac{1}{2}$ piece is larger than the $\frac{1}{4}$ piece.
   This is because the first pie was cut into fewer, and therefore larger, pieces.

2. a) $\frac{2}{7}$

   b) $\frac{10}{11}$

   c) $\frac{1}{4}$

3. a) $\frac{8}{15}$

   b) $\frac{7}{6}$

   c) $\frac{3}{10}$

4. a) $\frac{5}{8}$

   b) $\frac{4}{15}$

   c) $\frac{4}{6}$

   d) $\frac{9}{20}$

   e) $\frac{1}{10}$

   f) $\frac{3}{12}$

5. a) $\frac{6}{10}$

   b) $\frac{7}{6}$

   c) $\frac{4}{12}$

F-8 HW

1. a) $\frac{2}{15}$

   b) $\frac{4}{6}$

   c) $\frac{4}{7}$

   d) $\frac{7}{20}$

   e) $\frac{4}{9}$

---

f) $\frac{1}{6}$

g) $\frac{5}{12}$

h) $\frac{13}{25}$

i) $\frac{6}{11}$

2. a) $\frac{1}{5}$

   b) $\frac{1}{3}$

   c) $\frac{1}{2}$

   d) $\frac{1}{4}$

   e) $\frac{1}{2}$

   f) $\frac{?}{3}$

   g) $\frac{1}{4}$

   h) $\frac{1}{3}$

3. a) $\frac{2}{3}$

   b) $\frac{3}{4}$

   c) $\frac{2}{3}$

   d) $\frac{4}{5}$

   e) $\frac{2}{3}$

   f) $\frac{1}{2}$

   g) $\frac{4}{5}$

   h) $\frac{2}{5}$

4. a) $\frac{6}{6} = 1$

   b) $\frac{9}{15} = \frac{3}{5}$

   BONUS:

   c) $\frac{4}{6} = \frac{2}{3}$

   d) $\frac{7}{8}$

F-12 HW

1. a) $\frac{5}{6}$

   b) $\frac{1}{4}$

   c) $\frac{3}{11}$

---

d) $\frac{13}{20}$

e) $\frac{4}{9}$

f) $\frac{6}{25}$

2. a) $\frac{7}{6}$

b) $\frac{4}{11}$

3. a) $\frac{5}{2}$

b) $\frac{10}{3}$

c) $\frac{17}{3}$

d) $\frac{17}{5}$

e) $\frac{21}{5}$

f) $\frac{31}{6}$

4. a) 3 R1

b) 4 R1

c) 3 R2

d) 5 R2

e) 1 R3

f) 1 R2

5. a) $3\frac{1}{2}$

b) $3\frac{2}{3}$

c) $3\frac{2}{5}$

d) $5\frac{1}{4}$

Answer Key:
Practice Test – Level C

1. a) $\frac{3}{8}$
   b) $\frac{2}{5}$
2. a) $\frac{3}{7}$
   b) $\frac{4}{5}$
   c) $\frac{8}{11}$
   d) $\frac{13}{10}$
   e) $\frac{5}{6}$
   f) $\frac{6}{10}$
   g) $\frac{2}{9}$
   h) $\frac{6}{6} = 1$
3. a) $\frac{1}{3}$
   b) $\frac{2}{3}$
   c) $\frac{1}{3}$
   d) $\frac{4}{5}$
4. a) $2\frac{2}{3}$
   b) $3\frac{1}{2}$
5. a) $\frac{4}{3}$
   b) $\frac{11}{4}$
6. a)
   b)
7. a)
   b)

Final Test – Level C

1. a) $\frac{1}{3}$
   b) $\frac{3}{10}$
2. a) $\frac{3}{5}$
   b) $\frac{4}{11}$
   c) $\frac{8}{17}$
   d) $\frac{5}{6}$
   e) $\frac{8}{15}$
   f) $\frac{4}{6} = \frac{2}{3}$
   g) $\frac{2}{9}$
   h) $\frac{8}{10} = \frac{4}{5}$
3. a) $\frac{1}{5}$
   b) $\frac{2}{3}$
   c) $\frac{1}{3}$
   d) $\frac{4}{5}$
4. a) $1\frac{2}{3}$
   b) $2\frac{1}{2}$
5. a) $\frac{7}{3}$
   b) $\frac{15}{4}$
6. a)
   b)
7. a)
   b)

Practice Test – Level D

1. a) $\frac{3}{8}$
   b) $\frac{2}{5}$
2. a) $\frac{3}{7}$
   b) $\frac{4}{5}$
   c) $\frac{2}{11}$
   d) $\frac{13}{10}$
   e) $\frac{5}{6}$
   f) $\frac{6}{10} = \frac{3}{5}$
   g) $\frac{2}{9}$
   BONUS:
   h) $\frac{6}{6} = 1$
3. a) $\frac{1}{3}$
   b) $\frac{2}{3}$
   c) $\frac{1}{3}$
   d) $\frac{4}{5}$
4. a) $\frac{10}{3}$
   b) $\frac{8}{5}$
5. a) $3\frac{1}{2}$
   b) $2\frac{2}{3}$
6. a) $\frac{23}{6} = 3\frac{5}{6}$
   b) $\frac{19}{6} = 3\frac{1}{6}$
7. a) $\frac{1}{2}$
   b) $\frac{4}{5}$
8. Together they ate $\frac{5}{8}$ of the pizza.

Final Test – Level D

1. a) $\frac{1}{4}$
   b) $\frac{3}{10}$
2. a) $\frac{4}{8} = \frac{1}{2}$
   b) $\frac{2}{5}$
   c) $\frac{7}{12}$
   d) $\frac{9}{10}$
   e) $\frac{13}{15}$
   f) $\frac{6}{12} = \frac{1}{2}$
   g) $\frac{10}{20} = \frac{1}{2}$
   BONUS:
   h) $\frac{9}{15} = \frac{3}{5}$
3. a) $\frac{1}{4}$
   b) $\frac{2}{3}$
   c) $\frac{1}{4}$
   d) $\frac{3}{5}$
4. a) $\frac{9}{2}$
   b) $\frac{12}{5}$
5. a) $2\frac{1}{3}$
   b) $4\frac{1}{2}$
6. a) $\frac{19}{6} = 3\frac{1}{6}$
   b) $\frac{23}{15} = 1\frac{8}{15}$
7. a) $\frac{4}{9}$
   b) $\frac{3}{5}$
8. Together they ate $\frac{14}{15}$ of the pizza.

APPENDIX: Basic Operations

Addition (Where one number is a single digit)

Example: 16 + 3 =

Step 1:   Say the greater number (16) with your fist closed.

Step 2:   Count up by ones raising first your thumb, then one finger at a time until you have the same number of fingers up as the lower number.

Step 3:   The number you say when you have the second number of fingers up is the answer (in this case you say 19 when you have three fingers up, so 19 is the sum of 16 & 3)

A great bonus question would be to add a multi-digit number to a single-digit number (e.g. 1653 + 8). Just make sure your student can count high numbers.

Subtraction (Where the answer is a single digit)

Example: 11 – 8 =

Step 1:   Say the lesser number (8) with your fist closed.

Step 2:   Count up by ones raising first your thumb, then one finger at a time until you have reached the higher number (11).

Step 3:   The number of fingers you have up when you reach the final number is the answer (in this case you have three fingers up, so three is the difference between 8 & 11)

A great bonus question would be double- or triple-digit subtractions whose difference is a single digit (e.g. 462 – 458). Just make sure your student can count high numbers.